The
Illustrated
Encyclopaedia
'Ugly'
of
Animals

THE ILLUSTRATED ENCYCLOPAEDIA OF 'UGLY' ANIMALS

Sami Bayly

wren
&rook

Published in Great Britain in 2020 by Wren & Rook
First published in Australia and New Zealand in 2019 by Hachette Australia

Copyright © Samantha Bayley, 2019
Published by arrangement with Hachette Australia
All rights reserved.

The right of Samantha Bayley to be identified as the author and illustrator of this Work has
been asserted by her in accordance with the Copyright, Designs and Patents Act 1988

ISBN: 978 1 5263 6304 6
E-book ISBN: 978 1 5263 6305 3
10 9 8 7 6 5 4 3 2 1

Wren & Rook
An imprint of
Hachette Children's Group
Part of Hodder & Stoughton
Carmelite House
50 Victoria Embankment
London EC4Y 0DZ

An Hachette UK Company
www.hachette.co.uk
www.hachettechildrens.co.uk

Printed in China

Contents

Introduction

7

Introduction

The Illustrated Encyclopaedia of 'Ugly' Animals is a celebration of the beauty in 'ugliness'.

Regardless of whether or not we find these animals appealing to look at, they play an important role in our environment. The attributes that we see as 'ugly' almost always have a purpose or function that the animals have adapted over many years to assist them throughout their lives and with their survival.

Ugliness is, of course, subjective. It was through painting these sixty animals in scientific detail that I truly discovered the beauty they all encompass. I don't believe our contemporary human definition of 'ugliness' can be applied to the animal kingdom (just as it should not be applied to our own society).

Whilst researching these weird and wonderful species, I quickly discovered how many of them were in fact endangered or falling critically low in population, and that without them our amazing and diverse ecosystems would cease to function.

I hope that by the end of this book you will find your perception of beauty challenged, learn something new to tell your family or friends, and most importantly, find an 'ugly' creature to love.

Sami Bayly

Inia geoffrensis

Amazon River Dolphin

Inia geoffrensis
(in-e-a geo-fren-sis)

Description

These tubby, pinkish dolphins can reach a length of 2.5 metres for males and 2 metres for females. They get pinker as they get older and it is thought they developed this adaptation to match the muddy waters of their surroundings. Another possibility is that due to excessive fighting, their scar tissue begins to show through, developing a pinker tinge.

The noticeable bulge on their heads is used for echolocation. The dolphins send out sounds through the water, which bounce back to them when they hit something. The returning sounds are processed through the lump. This technique helps the dolphins work out the size and distance of potential prey. Their chubby necks allow them to turn their heads up to 90 degrees in any direction, which helps them when hunting for food.

Conservation Status

DATA DEFICIENT

Due to the lack of recent research into the Amazon river dolphin, their population size and trends are not well understood. They have been recorded as abundant in some areas, but this is not a reliable measure of their numbers as it doesn't take into account the full range of their habitat.

Despite this lack of information, it is clear these dolphins face threats from humans, for example when fishermen accidently catch them, or destroy their habitat through netting. They have even been used as bait or deliberately killed because they eat the other fish that fishermen want to catch.

A technique called 'explosive fishing' has been used in rivers containing these dolphins. It involves throwing bombs into the water to kill fish and has had a negative impact on the dolphins.

Local people are reluctant to hunt the Amazon river dolphin and will only utilise their body parts if they find a dolphin that is already dead. When this happens, they use the dolphin's fat and oil for medicinal remedies, and their teeth and eyes as love charms.

Diet

These mammals survive on any species of fish they find near the riverbed, but they have also been known to use their sharp teeth to eat turtles, crabs and even piranhas!

Location/Habitat

Like their name suggests, these dolphins are found in the Amazon River, which runs through Brazil, Colombia and Peru. They can also be found in the Orinoco River, running through Colombia and Venezuela. It is possible their distribution extends to rivers in Bolivia and Ecuador too. Amazon river dolphins enjoy tropical freshwater rivers, ponds and lakes. They also spend time in forest areas that flood during rainy seasons.

Fun Facts

→ Amazon river dolphins are known as being very inquisitive and friendly, even playing with local kids in the water.

→ They were thought to be blind because of their tiny eyes. In fact, they utilise them and have even been known to gaze into a human's eyes when confronted.

→ They are the largest river dolphin species.

→ Female dolphins are called 'cows' and males are known as 'bulls'.

American Manatee

Trichechus manatus
(tri-kek-us man-a-tus)

Description

This slow-moving, docile sea cow may appear to have missed out in the beauty department, especially with its pudgy, hairy body, paddle-shaped flippers and wrinkly, grey skin covered in algae. However, all of these 'misfortunes' are actually adaptations that make the manatee better suited to its environment and diet. Their paddle-shaped limbs come in handy to help propel them along the sea floor, so they use less energy while travelling and feeding. Their skin ensures they blend into their environment, protecting them from predators.

The bristly hairs on their bodies and around their mouths are sensory features which help them assess their surroundings through vibrations in the water. American manatees rely on this adaptation because of their poor eyesight. These hefty mammals will reach up to 2.5 metres and weigh in at an average of 200–600 kilograms.

Conservation Status

VULNERABLE

The biggest threat facing the American manatee is human. Due to their large size and the fact that they live in shallow, sometimes highly populated waters, manatees are frequently struck by negligent boat drivers. Manatees are also hunted for their skin, bones and by-products.

Close Relations

Although manatees are water dwellers, they are closely related to elephants. However, when they were first seen by the colonist and explorer Christopher Columbus, he thought he was looking at the mythical mermaid.

Diet

American manatees use their malleable top lips to feed on a variety of sea grasses, algae, roots and mangroves. They use this separated-lip adaptation to isolate individual plants and uproot them from the ground. The manatee does not have a typical set of teeth but only some molars at the back of their jaw. These will regrow when they become worn down.

Location/Habitat

There are four subpopulations which make up the American manatee population, all of which are found in Florida and Georgia in the United States. They are also sometimes found in South American countries, such as Mexico and the Bahamas. Like other migratory animals, manatees travel to find warmer water as the seasons change. They live at depths ranging 0.4–6 metres, in channels, canals, creeks, lagoons and seagrass beds.

Fun Facts

→ American manatees can feed for up to 8 hours a day, consuming an average of 33 kilograms of food. That's a lot of seagrass!

→ Pirates would eat dried manatee meat, known as 'buccan', so often that they later became known as 'buccaneers'.

→ Since they are mammals, manatees must hold their breath while underwater. Although the average submersion time is 4 minutes, they can stay under for up to 18!

Trichechus manatus

Eulagisca gigantea

Antarctic Scale Worm

Eulagisca gigantea

(yool-a-gis-ka gi-gant-e-a)

Description

Antarctic scale worms are 20-centimetre-long marine worms belonging to a class called *polychaetes*, more commonly known as bristle worms. It is not known exactly what purpose the brush-like bristles on their sides serve, but there are a number of suggested functions related to defending themselves against predators, helping them move across seabeds or assisting in swimming. From a distance, they appear to be beautiful creatures with an intricate, gold ribbon-like appearance. But on closer examination, they're actually quite terrifying!

The scale worm's most incredible evolutionary adaptation is what appears to be its 'head'. What looks like an eyeless face is actually a retractable mouth. Scale worms keep this mouth tucked away and covered up and will expel it from their body only when feeding.

Conservation Status

NOT EVALUATED

Very little is known about the scale worm's conservation status or the potential threats to its survival. Due to their deep-sea habitat, it is believed that scale worms are threatened by similar dangers as blobfish and batfish (found on pages 37 and 98), for example trawling or changes in water temperature due to global warming.

Diet

As they reside in deep-sea waters, there is little information known about their diet or feeding methods and habits. Scientists assume they feed on other deep-sea animals, but it is unclear which ones. Because of their large mouth and teeth, it is thought they are quick and aggressive hunters. Fortunately, they pose no threat to humans because we cannot reach their habitats unless we are in heavily protected equipment, like submarines.

Location/Habitat

Scale worms are usually found in hydrothermal vents in the Southern Ocean waters near Antarctica.

Fun Facts

→ The teeth-like scales that cover the scale worm's body are known as elytra.

→ Scale worms were first discovered in 1939 and were put on the World Register of Marine Species, but not much has been documented about them since.

→ Their class, *polychaetes*, is named for the Latin phrase 'many bristles'.

→ The collective name for a group of worms is a bed.

→ Scale worms are a recent discovery and it is now thought there could be around 16,000 undiscovered species of marine worms, compared with the 8,000 of them that are known.

Asian Sheepshead Wrasse

Semicossyphus reticulatus

(semi-kos-e-fus re-tik-you-la-tus)

Description

The most noticeable feature of the wrasse is their bulbous head and chin. While very little is known about the purpose of these bony growths, it is suspected they might be useful in attracting a mate during breeding season.

Another incredible attribute is that a female can change into a male halfway through her life. The purpose behind this is still not fully understood, but scientists believe it is an evolutionary solution to reduce the risk of population decline by ensuring that there will always be a mate to reproduce with.

The Asian sheepshead wrasse has been recorded to reach a massive 1 metre long and can weigh up to 14.7 kilograms.

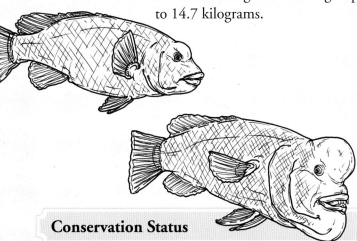

Conservation Status

DATA DEFICIENT

There is little information about this species of wrasse but we do know the population is dwindling. It is likely that overfishing will negatively impact the population size of the Asian sheepshead wrasse if no limitations are put in place.

Recent research suggests household chemicals, if poured into a drain, can end up in the ocean and may have an effect on the reproduction rates and sexual organs of these fish.

Diet

Not a lot is known about the food sources of this wrasse species, but crustaceans and shellfish are thought to make up the majority of their diet. This could explain their unusual teeth, which are perfect for chewing through or opening shells.

Location/Habitat

Asian sheepshead wrasse are found in the cool seas surrounding Japan, China, North and South Korea. However, even there they are not commonly seen.

Fun Facts

→ The term for animals that can change genders is 'sequential hermaphrodites'. It is mostly fish and gastropods that can do this.

→ Data retrieved by scientists about this species can be unreliable as what is documented as female one day may be documented as male another.

→ Wrasse that are born female can develop into even larger male fish than wrasse that are born male.

Semicossyphus reticulatus

Periophthalmus barbarus

Atlantic Mudskipper

Periophthalmus barbarus

(peer-e-off-thal-mus bar-ba-rus)

Description

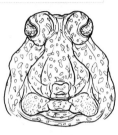

This territorial, amphibious fish is quite the looker. Their brown, slimy bodies can reach 15 centimetres long. Their shape has evolved to assist the mudskippers in crawling onto land for protection from predators, while also allowing them to live underwater.

The mudskippers' pectoral fins are shaped like limbs and enable them to effectively walk onto rocks and sand outside of the water. Perhaps the most interesting aspect of their powerful bodies is what gives them their name. Using their long tails as a springboard, they can propel themselves forward in a jumping or skipping motion which helps them to both escape predators and get around.

Another interesting aspect of the Atlantic mudskipper is their eyes, which sit on the top of their heads, allowing them a 360-degree view of the world.

Conservation Status

LEAST CONCERN

Fortunately for the Atlantic mudskipper, their population is under very little threat. They also have a large, wide-spread range which means they are of least concern in terms of conservation.

Diet

Since this animal is able to hunt for food underwater and on land, they can be found feasting on a range of arthropods (an invertebrate with an internal skeleton) and crustaceans, such as insects, worms and crabs.

Location/Habitat

Incredibly, the Atlantic mudskipper has evolved to live both in the water and out. On land, their gills close, keeping some water with them and activating an internal oxygenated chamber to ensure they can breathe. They are found along the west African coast or on the islands of the Gulf of Guinea, and prefer muddy, shallow fresh waters and the nearby platforms and rocks. They will spend their days darting back and forth between the water and land, keeping themselves wet and hydrated while searching for food.

Fun Facts

- In order to keep their eyes moist when outside of the water, Atlantic mudskippers have a flap of skin over their eyeballs to protect them.
- During mating season, the males become more vibrant in colour.
- Males that live close to one another are quite competitive and will act aggressively towards each other, sometimes resulting in the death of one of them.
- There are 15 species of mudskipper, and the Atlantic Ocean has the largest population.
- Their scientific name, *Periophthalmus*, refers to their ability to see 360 degrees, and translates to 'round eye'.

Atlantic Trumpetfish

Aulostomus strigosus
(awl-os-toe-mus strig-osus)

Description

The Atlantic trumpetfish is able to lure unsuspecting prey by changing colour to blend in with the environment.

Their long, thin bodies can reach lengths of 1 metre and are ideally shaped to help them blend in with seagrass while floating vertically upside down. This comes in handy both as a means of hiding from predators and in helping them hunt for food.

Conservation Status

LEAST CONCERN

Although the Atlantic trumpetfish has a substantial range and is considered of least concern from a conservation perspective, this species lost a large percentage of its environment in the 1970s due to large-scale coral loss caused by humans. While there are measures currently in place to protect the Atlantic trumpetfish, it is important to be aware our actions can have devastating effects on the world around us.

Diet

While it may look like these trumpetfish have a long mouth, it is actually a very long face. They have a small mouth at the end of this face and hunt by waiting until the last moment before pouncing on their prey, their mouths extending forward to suction up the unsuspecting meal. Because of this little mouth, Atlantic trumpetfish feed on small creatures like invertebrates and fish, which can be easily suctioned in.

Location/Habitat

Atlantic trumpetfish like to live at depths of approximately 4–25 metres in clear waters surrounded by coral and reefs. They can be found in the western Atlantic Ocean, for example around south Florida, the Bahamas, the Gulf of Mexico and Bermuda.

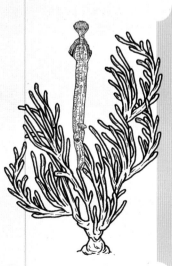

Fun Facts

- Atlantic trumpetfish get their name from their long bodies which are thought to look like trumpets.
- Lionfish are a major negative influence on the survival of the Atlantic trumpetfish because they are causing a lot of destruction to native sea plants and corals.
- They have spines down their backs which they raise when defending themselves from predators.
- As with sea horses, male Atlantic trumpetfish carry and care for the eggs in a small pouch until they are ready to be born.
- This species is also often referred to as the 'painted flutemouth', another musical instrument reference.

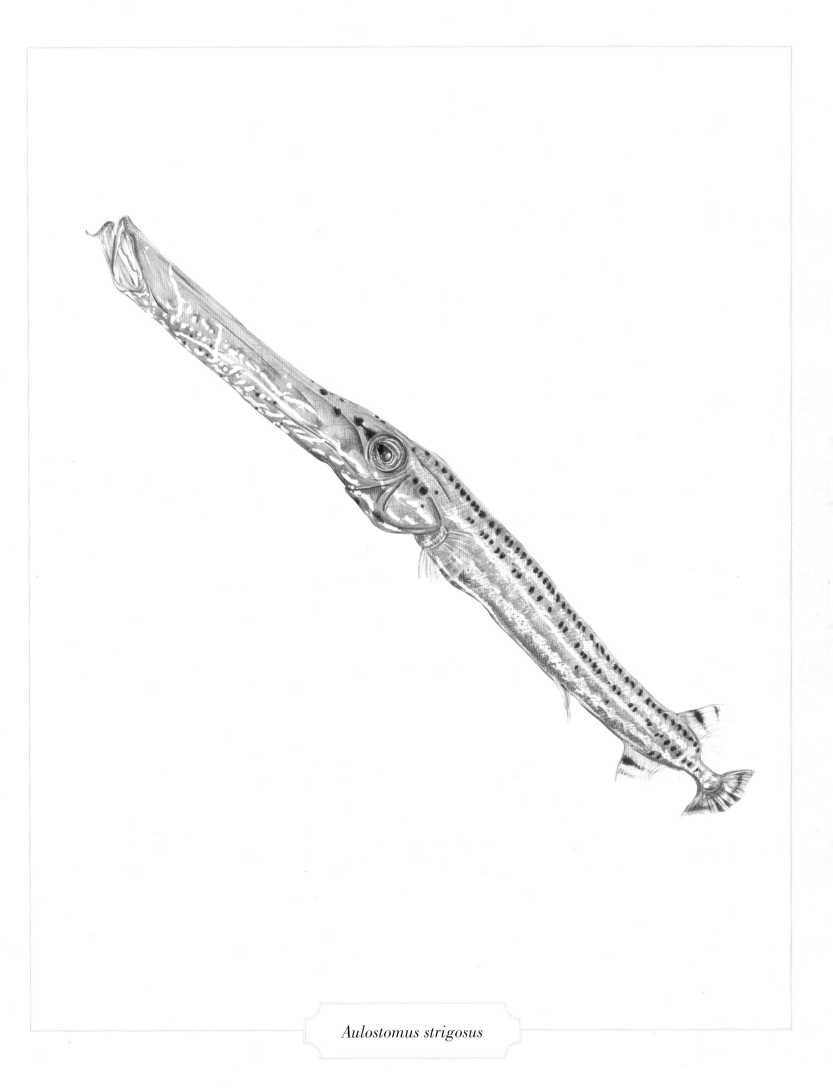

Aulostomus strigosus

Alectura lathami

Australian Brush-turkey

Alectura lathami

(a-lek-tura lar-thar-me)

Description

Like other species of turkey, Australian brush-turkeys feature an unflattering, wrinkled neck pouch, known as a wattle. These turkeys are sexually dimorphic, which means males and females display different physical features, and their wattles are much larger in the males. They are yellow most of the time but have been known to change colour in relation to their location and age. For example, in Northern Queensland in Australia, they are more of a pale blue colour.

They have large, powerful feet and claws that allow them to dig up the earth. They are part of the megapode family, which is a group of around 22 large-footed, fowl-like birds.

Conservation Status

LEAST CONCERN

It is thought that there are over 100,000 individual brush-turkeys, and despite excessive hunting by humans during the Great Depression in the 1930s, their numbers are currently very strong.

Today, the main threats to the brush-turkey population are foxes and cats, goannas eating their eggs and humans encroaching on their habitats.

Close Relations

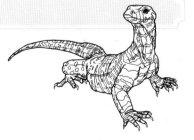

They are related to the wild turkey, found on page 127.

Diet

Using their powerful feet, brush-turkeys will search for food like insects, fruit and seeds under the earth. Unfortunately, this method of foraging is a large part of the reason they are seen as such an annoyance in rural Australia, as they will often visit neatly kept gardens and destroy them in just one short feeding session.

Location/Habitat

Like its name suggests, the Australian brush-turkey can be found within Australia, from New South Wales to Far North Queensland. They live in shrub-like environments, rainforests and other coastal forestry surroundings.

Fun Facts

⤳ Male brush-turkeys can make nests as large as a car!

⤳ If you would like to keep them out of your yard, it is best to do so by removing any sign of a nest and by hiding any food left outside for your pets, as brush-turkeys have been known to eat pet food.

⤳ Chicks are self-sufficient and can care for themselves only a few hours after hatching.

⤳ The Australian brush-turkey is the largest of all megapodes.

⤳ Their family, the megapodiidae, dates back 30 million years.

Australian Ghost Shark

Callorhinchus milii

(kal-or-inkus mil-e-eye)

Description

The Australian ghost shark is known by a few different names. As well as ghost sharks, they are also called 'elephant fish', 'whitefish' and 'plownose chimaeras'. These names all refer to the adaptations this species has developed, for example its long, large nose which is coated in sensory pores that detect electrical fields and movement to help the fish find its prey. This is useful for finding food hidden in layers of sand and dirt.

Conservation Status

LEAST CONCERN

The unusual-looking ghost shark is regularly farmed by humans and is also the target of ocean-dwelling predators such as sharks.

Due to overfishing within Australian waters, limitations were put in place to try and prevent any further drop in their numbers. In Victoria, for example, you can only catch one per day.

It's not just the fact that fish are being caught that has a negative impact on their numbers. The machinery and equipment used to retrieve them often destroys the environment around them.

Ghost sharks can also fall victim to the parasites *Gyrocotyle rugosa* and *Callorhynchicola multitesticulatus*, which, depending on the level of infestation, can cause physical impairment, mechanical damage and harm to reproductive ability.

Diet

Ghost sharks are carnivorous and use their trunk-like nose to plough across sandy ocean floors in search of food, such as other fish, molluscs, clams, worms and shellfish.

Location/Habitat

When they are young, these unusual fish can be found inhabiting estuaries and shallow coastal waters off South Australia and New Zealand. When they are older, they travel to deeper waters of up to 200 metres.

Fun Facts

→ Ghost sharks are a common ingredient in fish and chips in both New Zealand and Australia.

→ Their eggs – which take 8 months to hatch – are very oddly shaped. They have a leathery texture and can reach 25 centimetres long.

→ Ghost sharks can reach 15 years of age.

→ Like sharks, they have a cartilage skeleton instead of one made of bone.

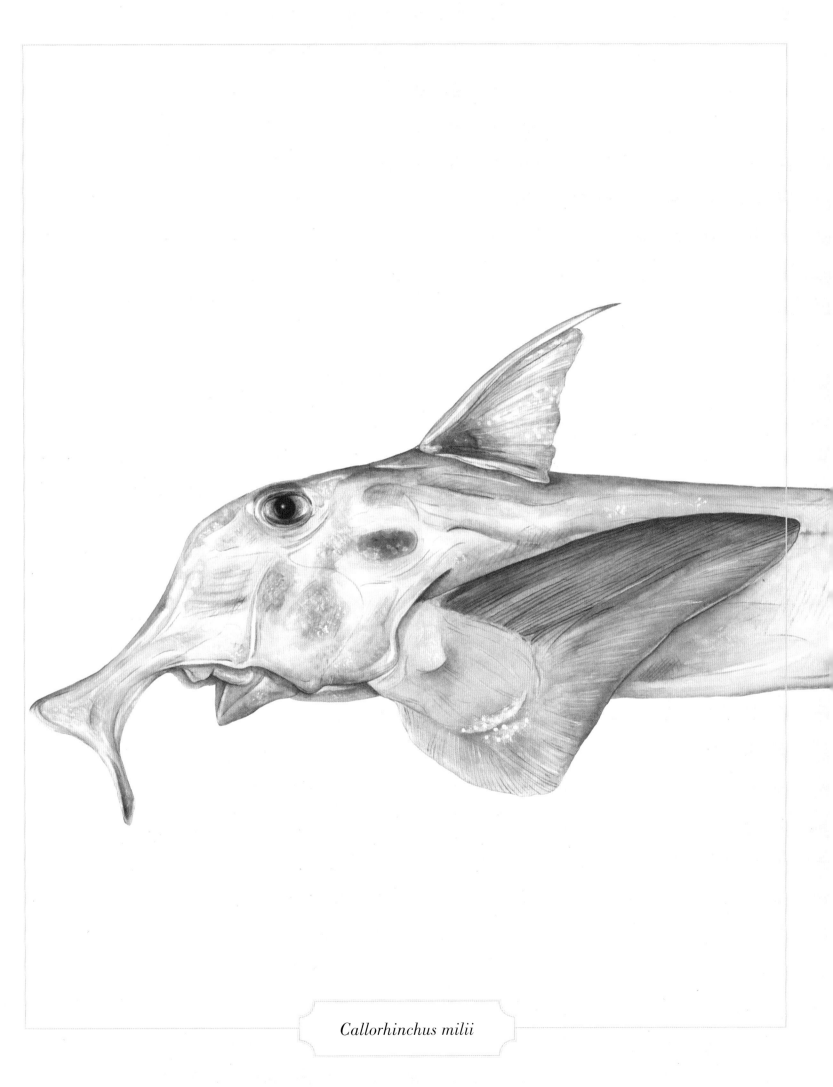

Callorhinchus milii

Threskiornis moluccus

Australian White Ibis

Threskiornis moluccus

(thres-key-or-nis mol-uk-us)

Description

As with the northern bald ibis, this bird has a naked, featherless head. This is probably to minimise the grooming time required after eating messy meals, as well as to stop the spread of pathogens.

These ibis have a patch of red skin at the back of their bald necks and on the underside of their wings, which becomes more vibrant during breeding season. In their natural habitats, they are covered in white feathers, although with more time spent in dirty, rubbish-filled environments, they easily become brown and soiled.

Conservation Status

LEAST CONCERN

The Australian white ibis faces threats such as habitat loss, pest-driven hunting and the general effects of a poor diet due to their proximity to human populations. It has been found that approximately 50% of these birds are forced to eat from landfill each day. Luckily for this ibis, however, their numbers are stable, and they are not considered to be of concern when it comes to conservation.

Close Relations

As you can probably tell, these birds are closely related to the northern bald ibis on page 89. It's not just their names that are similar – they also look alike, with both birds featuring hairless heads and long, thin beaks.

Diet

Ibis beaks have evolved to be wonderful tools for eating creatures like insects and mussels that live down holes or tunnels, and for hammering the shells against hard rocks to crack them open, gobbling down the insides. However, as a result of changes to their habitat, you are more likely to see them using their beaks to reach into bins and pull out food scraps than to crack open shellfish.

Location/Habitat

The Australian white ibis used to inhabit wetlands throughout Queensland in Australia and all the way down to Victoria. However, as so much of their habitat has been destroyed to make way for human expansion, it is now more common to see these birds in highly populated city environments.

Fun Facts

→ You may have heard these birds called by other names such as bin chicken, trash turkey or flying rat.

→ During courtship, males will perform a wonderful routine to entice the female. He will then gift her a small twig and the two will groom one another. How romantic!

→ Certain councils across Australia have permits to cull the birds because they are seen as pests.

→ There were approximately 9,000 ibis counted in Sydney in 2014.

Aye-aye

Daubentonia madagascariensis
(door-ben-toe-ne-a mada-gaskar-e-en-sis)

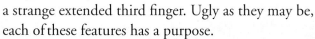

Description

Aye-ayes have enormous ears and a piercing gaze. Their front teeth are long and sharp, and they have a strange extended third finger. Ugly as they may be, each of these features has a purpose.

As they are nocturnal, aye-ayes have developed wide-set eyes to ensure clearer vision in the dark. These primates put their ears to unusual use when looking for food. They cup them around tree trunks and branches while tapping their elongated fingers quickly against the wood. In this way they are able to hear where the hollow sections are. They use their teeth to gnaw holes into the bark, which they then stretch their long middle fingers into. They are able to pierce grubs and insects with their hook-like nail and drag them out to eat. This technique is called 'percussive foraging' and aye-ayes are one of only a few species to use it.

Conservation Status

ENDANGERED

According to local superstition in Madagascar, the aye-aye is a sign of bad luck or death. They are often killed if spotted during the night and then hung by their tails along the roadside. It is hoped passers-by will take the bad luck with them as they leave. Another key threat to their survival is habitat loss as trees and land are being cleared in order to make houses, boats and other wooden objects.

Close Relations

While these small animals might look like rodents, they are actually part of the primate family and are related to apes and chimpanzees.

Diet

The aye-aye uses its elongated, multi-use finger to scoop out liquids and insects from coconuts and trees. Ninety per cent of their diet is made up of tree growths, fruit and nectar. They also eat large quantities of insect larvae, which provides protein and fat to their diet.

Location/Habitat

Found across the coasts of Madagascar, the aye-aye likes to live in forests and plantations, as well as in swampy mangroves. During the day, they hide up in the canopy but are active during the night, spending the safe hours of darkness hunting for food in the tree tops.

Fun Facts

> There is an old superstition that if an aye-aye points at you with its long middle finger, you will die.

> They have the largest brains among the prosimians, a group of many different primate species which also includes lemurs.

> Their name is thought to come from the sound they make when startled – 'hai-hai'.

> They have been documented to live for up to 23 years in captivity.

Daubentonia madagascariensis

Cacajao calvus

Bald-headed Uakari

Cacajao calvus

(caka-jow cal-vus)

Description

The bald-headed uakari's bright red face and hairless head looks strange to humans, but is a desired look among other uakaris. Crimson cheeks signal health and attract female uakaris to mate. A paler complexion is a turn-off for potential mates as it implies sickness or a possible malaria infection, which is common among the species.

They are smart, playful and communal monkeys, frequently displaying their emotions and thoughts through facial expressions and sounds.

Location/Habitat

Bald-headed uakaris are found in the forests of Brazil and Peru, in low-density areas near a water source. They feel safer among the trees since they are arboreal, but can be spotted more easily than other monkeys because of their vibrant colours.

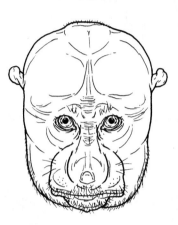

Conservation Status

VULNERABLE

Because of their human-like features, bald-headed uakaris are not regularly hunted, yet they still face threats which make the species vulnerable. Land clearing is the leading cause of their declining numbers because these uakaris climb from tree to tree to avoid seasonal flooding.

Diet

The uakaris spend most of their feeding time high up in trees, where they eat leaves, nuts, fruit and insects. Occasionally they climb down to the forest floor to feast on dropped fruits and seeds. They will split up to find food during the day, and regather at night for safety in numbers.

Fun Facts

→ The collective name for a group of uakaris is a troop.

→ The correct way to pronounce their name is 'wakari'.

→ They only give birth once every two years.

→ They rely on using their arms and legs to get them across the tree branches, as their tail is small and stumpy.

→ The reason their faces are so red is because they only have a thin layer of skin covering their capillaries. The red you can see is actually flowing blood!

Black Musselcracker

Cymatoceps nasutus

(sym-a-toe-seps nay-suh-tus)

Description

This is not your ordinary small coral fish. Black musselcrackers can reach 130 centimetres long and weigh up to 45 kilograms.

Their human-like faces feature plump, nose-like snouts and a mouth full of powerful teeth. These teeth are how they get their name: 'musselcracker'.

Another extremely interesting adaptation they have is the ability to change sex from female to male – similar to the Asian sheepshead wrasse featured on page 14). This unusual skill is known as hermaphroditism, and most commonly occurs in females when they reach maturity at approximately 18 years of age and 70 centimetres long. There are a number of theories as to why this happens, but it is most likely a way to ensure mating can take place and the species continue when there are few available males.

Conservation Status

VULNERABLE

Unfortunately, black musselcrackers are being over-exploited and their population is diminishing due to their status as trophy fish.

In order to reduce the rate of their falling numbers, there have been fishing limitations put in place, such as a minimum catch size of 50 centimetres and a limit of one catch per day.

Diet

Foods that appeal to the black musselcracker include crustaceans and molluscs, such as sea stars, crabs, sea urchins and anything with a hard shell or surface. Because of their strong jaws, they can use their molars and front teeth to crack the shells of their prey and consume the insides.

Location/Habitat

Found in the waters of South Africa and Mozambique, the adults reside in rocky reef environments approximately 100 metres deep, while the young prefer a shallow home in rock pools or ditches. They favour warm, clear waters and are quite sensitive to changes in water temperature.

Fun Facts

→ Their scientific name, *Cymatoceps nasutus,* translates from Latin to 'swollen head' and 'prominent nose'.

→ They have been recorded to grow as old as 45 years.

→ Their Afrikaans name is poenskop.

→ Unfortunately, parts of the black musselcracker are considered a delicacy in some areas of the world, meaning their catch rate is quite high.

→ The larger this fish grows, the more human-like its face looks!

Cymatoceps nasutus

Breviceps fuscus

Black Rain Frog

Breviceps fuscus
(brev-e-seps fuss-cus)

Description

Black rain frogs are covered in bumpy, wart-like spots and can have a strange, ballooned appearance and a sad-looking face. They are usually only 4–5 centimetres in length. Although they may look ridiculous, these features are actually part of their defence mechanism. In fact, they do not always look like this. It is only when they are feeling threatened or scared that they will puff themselves up in order to seem larger and more menacing. Doing this also prevents them from being pulled from their burrows, as once they are swollen, they cannot fit through the entrance.

Conservation Status

LEAST CONCERN

As well as threats from predators like pigs, snakes and birds of prey, black rain frogs are also negatively impacted by environmental issues. The habitats of these amphibians are beginning to deteriorate through the introduction of invasive plant species and frequent fires. Fortunately, these issues are being monitored to ensure the frogs' numbers do not fall too much.

Diet

Not much is known about the feeding habits of this species of frog. However, it is suspected they spend their days finding and eating worms, spiders and insects.

Location/Habitat

To find this species, you must travel to South Africa and to the forests and heathland areas of the southern tip, known as the Cape Fold Mountains. Since they are burrowing frogs, they do not spend their days in water, but instead can be found in tunnels as deep as 15 centimetres in the slopes and hills around the mountains.

Fun Facts

- The collective noun for black rain frogs is an army or a knot.
- These frogs are nocturnal, so are only active at night.
- The females lay around 43 eggs in their burrow. After this, they lay another mound of empty eggs on top. This means that the real babies are more likely to survive as when predators raid their burrows, they usually only eat the empty eggs on top.
- The male frogs stand guard over the eggs while waiting for them to hatch.

Black Snub-nosed Monkey

Rhinopithecus bieti

(ry-nop-ith-e-kus by-eti)

Description

What makes this monkey extra unusual is its upturned nose and plump, rosy lips. Its nose looks the way it does because it does not have a nasal bone, and its big lips cover large gums and teeth, which it displays when feeling threatened or scared.

The males weigh in at a rather heavy average of 14 kilograms and are 100–155 centimetres long including the tail. Females are smaller, reaching just over half the size of the males.

These monkeys have developed a range of calls and alarms to communicate with other monkeys, including light-hearted cheeps to show playfulness and barking to indicate rage, not to mention a number of calls to warn of oncoming danger.

Conservation Status

ENDANGERED

This is yet another one-of-a-kind primate species struggling to survive because of overwhelming deforestation, poaching and the impact of climate change on its habitat. Since the early 1980s, they have seen a 31% drop in distribution across the land. On top of this, black snub-nosed monkeys are frequently poisoned or caught in snares put down for other animals. There are plans to try and increase numbers by funding protected areas, promoting awareness and running breeding programs in China.

Diet

Black snub-nosed monkeys rely on fungus, algae, bamboo and the lichen on trees to give them energy throughout the day. In spring they also eat berries, insects, grass and flowers.

Location/Habitat

Another name for the black snub-nosed monkey is the Yunnan snub-nosed monkey. This is because they can be found in Yunnan, as well as in southwest China. They live in forests which are around 4,000 metres above sea level, where it is snowy almost every day of the year.

Fun Facts

→ Black snub-nosed monkeys are sexually dimorphic – for example, the males have longer fur than the females.

→ On average, these monkeys get 11 hours of sleep each night, sometimes even more in the colder months.

→ They are the only monkeys to live in habitats below 0 degrees Celsius for a long period of time.

→ When they go to sleep, they always arrange themselves so that the mothers and babies are in the middle, the other females are next, and the males are on the outside to guard against predators.

Rhinopithecus bieti

Psychrolutes microporos

Blobfish

Psychrolutes microporos
(sy-kro-loots micro-pore-os)

Description

The blobfish looks so disturbing because it has physically evolved to survive under very strong water pressure. It has little need for muscles or bones, since the depths where it lives can be 120 times the pressure at sea-level. Even though the blobfish looks strange to us, it is perfectly adapted for its environment. It weighs around 2 kilograms and can reach around 30 centimetres in length.

Conservation Status

NOT EVALUATED

There is very little known about the blobfish which was only discovered in 2003. It is thought that because of the conditions this fish was found to be living in, it has few predators and threats. The only major risk to the blobfish is human, through either deep-sea trawling nets, or effects from changing water temperatures due to global warming.

Close Relations

The blobfish is part of the psychrolutidae family, which also includes the toadfish.

Diet

Since they must conserve their minimal energy for daily tasks, the blobfish is presumed to feed on other slow-moving prey, such as sea snails, slugs, urchins and molluscs.

Location/Habitat

The first blobfish specimen was found off the coast of New Zealand. It was discovered 1,300 metres beneath the surface by a scientific research team of Australians and New Zealanders. It was given to the Australian Museum where 'Mr Blobby', as he is known, is now on display for educational purposes. The rest of the species can be found in the Indian, Pacific and Atlantic Oceans.

Fun Facts

- The blobfish's home is 2.5 times deeper than most submarines can reach.
- It is speculated that because of the slow aging process of deep-sea creatures, and the lack of predators, the blobfish can live to the incredible age of 130 years.
- Due to the changes of pressure and effects of the preservation process, Mr Blobby now looks slightly different from when he was originally found.
- Like the ocean sunfish on page 93, blobfish do not have a swim bladder, but instead rely on the natural buoyancy their skin provides.
- The blobfish was voted as the world's ugliest animal in 2013 by the Ugly Animal Preservation Society.

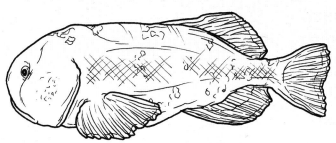

Pongo pygmaeus

Bornean Orangutan

Pongo pygmaeus
(pong-go pig-may-us)

Description

These primates are certainly not the most beautiful animals found in the world, but they are one of the most unusual!

Males have large cheek pads (known as flanges) on the sides of their faces, giving them a round, dinner-plate-like appearance. It is not known exactly what purpose these serve, although researchers have noted that the larger the flanges, the more attractive females will find a male.

The Bornean orangutan can weigh 60–90 kilograms and grow to 97 centimetres tall. They have abnormally long arms which can be up to 1 metre and help them to swing from tree to tree.

Conservation Status

CRITICALLY ENDANGERED

Unfortunately for the Bornean orangutan, due to mass habitat loss and poaching, their numbers are dropping fast. It is suspected there has been a loss of approximately 82% of the population since the 1940s, with a massive 2,256 orangutans killed in just one year in the Kalimantan region of Borneo. This, paired with their lengthy breeding process, means that Bornean orangutans are losing numbers much faster than they are gaining them and are therefore critically endangered.

Diet

Bornean orangutans are mostly herbivores, using their opposable thumbs to pick their food and sip water from rain caught in cupped leaves. Their diet consists mostly of plants, fruits and flowers. They also eat a range of insects and will sometimes feed on small mammals.

Location/Habitat

Each night, Bornean orangutans build nests high in the trees and out of reach of predators for them and their young to sleep in. To see them in the wild, you will have to visit the hilly forest zones in the Kalimantan, Sabah and Sarawak regions of Borneo.

Fun Facts

→ Bornean orangutans have been recorded to live as long as 60 years.

→ The word orangutan translates to 'man of the forest' in Malay and Indonesian.

→ Bornean orangutans cannot swim.

→ Humans share 97% of their DNA with these primates.

→ They are the largest tree-dwelling mammals in the world.

California Condor

Gymnogyps californianus
(gym-no-gips kali-forn-e-arnus)

Description

These enormous birds have a wingspan of up to 3 metres and weigh up to 14 kilograms. The males are typically larger than the females but have a similar colouration.

The California condor has a featherless head, showing off its wrinkly, pink skin and making it quite funny-looking. However, this adaptation saves them from having to clean their feathers after having a messy meal, which is useful as they already spend most of their day feeding and preening.

Conservation Status

CRITICALLY ENDANGERED

The California condor is unfortunately critically endangered due to mass hunting, habitat destruction and accidental lead poisoning from eating animals that farmers and locals used to shoot with lead bullets. This resulted in a huge number of California condor deaths.

Diet

They have a carrion diet which means they are mostly carnivorous, but they will generally not kill their food themselves. Instead, they flock to creatures that have already been killed by other animals or by cars, or have died naturally, such as cattle, deer and rabbits. This is of great benefit to the environment and ecosystem. They eat approximately 1.5 kilograms of carrion a day and this hurries along the process of decomposition and rids the area of germs.

Location/Habitat

They once occupied the length of the Pacific Coast of North America, but they can now only be found in south-central California. They enjoy living in rocky cliffs and tall trees from which they can scour the area for food, and also build nests for their young.

Fun Facts

- California condors will consume so much food that they cannot take flight for a few hours afterwards.
- They have been recorded to live to 60 years old.
- They can soar on the wind for up to an hour without needing to flap their wings once.
- The California condor is the biggest North American bird.
- They form life-long breeding pairs.

Gymnogyps californianus

Pelodiscus sinensis

Chinese Softshell Turtle

Pelodiscus sinensis

(pel-o-dis-kus si-nen-sis)

Description

The dark-olive, blotchy shells of these turtles are soft, like their name suggests, which is very uncommon among turtle species. While it doesn't offer the same protection as a hard shell, the soft shell allows them to move more smoothly and flexibly when travelling for long distances or on muddy floors. Their feet are webbed to make swimming easier.

This species of turtle is sexually dimorphic, with the female being larger (reaching around 30 centimetres long and weighing up to 6 kilograms) and having a more curved shell.

Close Relations

The Chinese softshell turtle is closely related to the spiny softshell turtle (Apalone spinifera), with the main physical difference being the small spines along their shells.

Most incredibly, they are capable of pharyngeal breathing. This means that they pump in water through their throat and intake oxygen from the water, allowing them to stay under the surface for lengthy periods.

Diet

These turtles are mostly carnivorous, eating small creatures like insects, worms, fish, and crustaceans. They will also eat leaves and aquatic vegetation.

Location/Habitat

Like most turtles, Chinese softshells love to inhabit the fresh and brackish waters of rivers, swamps, creeks and lakes. They are native to Japan, Vietnam and China but have been introduced to other pockets of Asia. They live in nests and will lay their eggs across the entrance of them. It generally takes 60 days for the eggs to hatch but this depends on the weather and temperature of each habitat.

Fun Facts

→ Although it may seem as though their shells are completely soft, they actually feature a solid bone in the middle, which helps the structure to remain rigid, while still being malleable.

→ Researchers are not sure exactly how long these turtles live but it is thought that they reach adulthood at around 4–6 years old.

→ This species of turtle is the most important when it comes to the Asian economy, as there are millions of them bred and sold for food each year.

→ On average they lay 8–30 eggs between two and five times each year.

Creatonotos gangis

Creatonotos gangis

(cree-a-ton-oat-os gang-gis)

Description

These moths have a red or yellow abdomen with dark-coloured front wings and lighter back wings. These are not its ugly feature, however. It is their weird feelers, known as coremata, which come out of their abdomen, that warrant their place on the list of ugly animals. These four appendages are usually retracted but will be pushed out during the breeding season to assist in the mating process. The coremata release chemicals known as pheromones that attract females and let them know they are ready to breed. Fully extended, they are larger than the moths' entire body, which can be up to 4 centimetres long.

Conservation Status

NOT EVALUATED

There is very little known about the *Creatonotos gangis'* conservation status. It is hoped that more research will be done on these moths in the future so we can better understand their population and the potential threats to their survival.

Diet

The diet of the *Creatonotos gangis* while in its caterpillar form, and sometimes during its moth stage, is mostly made up of plants that produce unusual chemicals called pyrrolizidine alkaloids (PAs).

Creatonotos gangis loves plants with these chemicals, which is strange as PAs are foul-tasting, toxic and deter almost all other insects and animals. For *Creatonotos gangis*, however, PAs are not only a tasty snack – they help the moths grow

their gangly coremata. The more PAs the caterpillars eat, the larger and more substantial their coremata will grow when they are moths. And the larger and more substantial their coremata, the better chance they have to mate.

Location/Habitat

If you are out and about in the Northern Territory, Western Australia and Queensland in Australia, or in Southeast Asia, you might come across the *Creatonotos gangis*. Their favourite plant hosts are pomegranate trees, rice, soybean and maize where they can eat enough PA-rich leaves.

Fun Facts

- *Creatonotos gangis* are also known as coremata, which is Greek for 'feather dusters'.
- They are not the only species of moth to have these long, hairy tentacles. In fact, even butterflies, like the highly admired African monarch, have this feature – only theirs are nowhere near as long or as noticeable.
- The pheromones released from male moths can spread as far as a few kilometres.
- Only female moths find the pheromones alluring. When male moths come across the scent, they are repelled and will immediately leave the scene.
- 3,000 hairs can be found on the coremata – imagine counting all that hair!

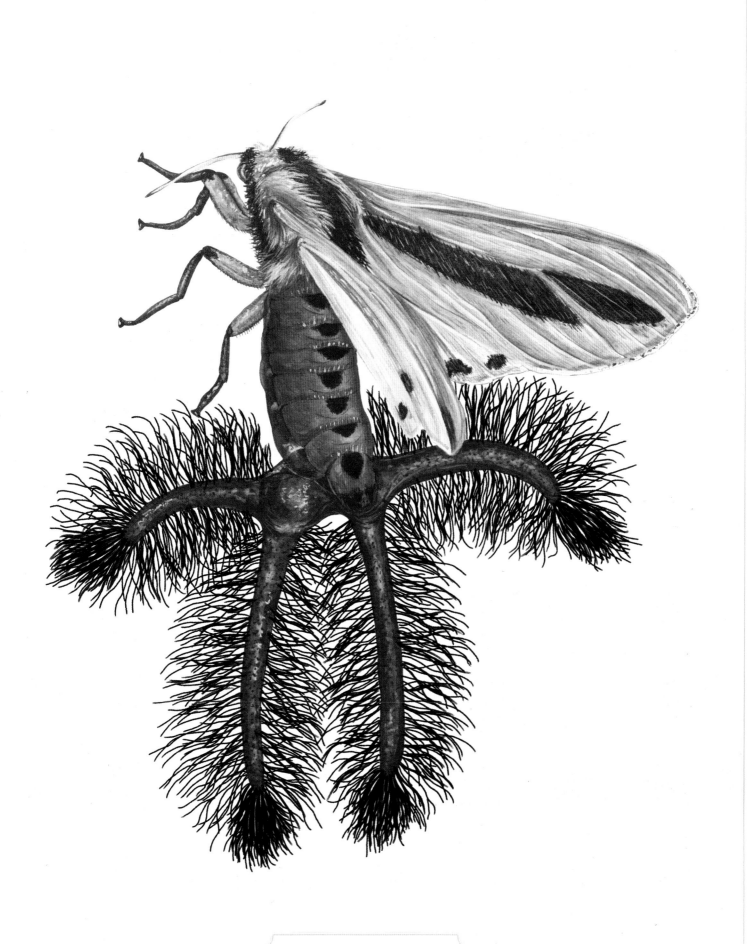

Creatonotos gangis

Enchelycore anatina

Fangtooth Moray

Enchelycore anatina
(en-chel-eye-core ana-tee-na)

Description

The most shocking aspect of the fangtooth moray's appearance is its icicle-like teeth, which grow to 2.5 centimetres and fill its large mouth in two rows. The first row is made up of the largest teeth, and the second contains the smaller teeth.

These teeth can cause a nasty bite and there are a few accounts of people experiencing this painful injury. It's not common though, as these moray eels are timid and peaceful, except when feeling extremely scared or threatened.

Their 120-centimetre, snake-like form, paired with a long dorsal fin, allows them to swim smoothly and quickly through the water, either to escape a threat or to chase their dinner.

Conservation Status

LEAST CONCERN

This species of moray eel is quite lucky – it has no known threats and is rarely impacted by humans. There could be a few reasons for this. For example, because they stay hidden for most of their lives, they might not come across many threats. They could also be intimidating to other animals and are therefore at the top of their food chain. Their menacing appearance certainly scares off humans whenever they come across them in the wild!

Diet

Their long, sharp teeth help them to bite and eat crustaceans, which make up the majority of their diet. Since they have poor eyesight and feed predominately at night, morays rely heavily on their sense of smell to find prey. They remain tucked inside their hideaways, only emerging to pounce on the small fish and crustaceans who swim by.

Location/Habitat

Quite difficult to find, these eels will stay hidden in rocky crevasses, corals and caves at depths of around 10–50 metres for most of their lives. They are quite common in the Atlantic Ocean, for example around the Canary Islands, Bermuda and Brazil. They can also be found in the Mediterranean Sea.

Fun Facts

→ Fangtooth morays are also known as tiger morays because of their black and yellow stripes.

→ It may seem like a threatening action, but by opening and closing their mouths and showing off their many teeth, fangtooth morays are actually pumping fresh water through their gills, helping them breathe.

→ Fangtooth moray eels have a symbiotic relationship with white striped cleaner shrimp. These small crustaceans will venture into an eel's mouth and clean its teeth of parasites and scraps which could damage the eel's teeth or health. The eel will not eat the shrimp and so both parties benefit from the relationship.

→ It is thought that this eel's range is expanding, since one has recently been found in the Aegean Sea.

Gelada Baboon

Theropithecus gelada
(thero-pith-e-kus gell-ada)

Description

These incredible creatures are known to use facial expressions to show how they feel and can display emotions like anger and playfulness, just like us! The most important expression to know is their warning look, telling you to back off. This is when their lips are pushed back over their gums and their canines are on display.

The deep red patch on their chests is also used in expression. These patches grow a deeper shade of red to signify that a female is ready to mate or to display a male's dominance. Incredibly, the male's chest patch will deepen or fade in colour in relation to his power over the herd – a truly extraordinary evolutionary adaptation.

Although both sexes have brown hair, males grow a magnificent mane and are usually larger than the females. They average around 125 centimetres tall and weigh around 20.5 kilograms, which is about 5 kilograms more than the females.

Conservation Status

LEAST CONCERN

Although the gelada's habitats are increasingly being destroyed to clear land for livestock and crops, these baboons are not considered at risk.

While there are some protections in place for this species of baboon, people are still allowed to hunt and kill them, and they are sometimes taken away from their habitats. These baboons are also often shot by humans who see them as pests for eating agricultural supplies. In the harsher seasons, they are even sometimes used for food.

Diet

Their terrifying long teeth suggest they're hunters, but in actual fact, geladas eat grass most of the time. They even use their human-like hands to pick single blades of grass from patches that they enjoy and will avoid the less tasty ones.

In drier months, they are forced to feed on roots, flowers, fruit and the occasional invertebrate, because the grasses they like have not seeded.

Location/Habitat

To see these baboons in their natural habitats, you must travel to Ethiopia and Eritrea. You will also need to climb steep cliffs, because these baboons like to huddle together in rocky gorges which they use as sleeping nooks. Even though they like to sleep in the cliffs, geladas are terrible climbers and spend most of their lives on the ground – they are what is known as terrestrial.

Fun Facts

> Gelada baboons have been recorded to live as long as 30 years in captivity but are suspected to live shorter lives in the wild.

> Aside from humans, geladas are the most ground-dwelling primates.

> Individual clans will consist of only one male with a number of females.

> The collective term for a group of geladas is a band or herd.

> They are one of the few species of ancient grazing primates that are still alive today.

Theropithecus gelada

Myrmecophaga tridactyla

Giant Anteater

Myrmecophaga tridactyla
(murm-e-cof-aga tri-dak-til-a)

Description

Giant anteaters have long snouts and fast-moving tongues. Reaching 2 metres from front to back and weighing up to 65 kilograms, giant anteaters use their sharp claws to slash open holes in ant and termite mounds before sticking their tubular noses down to collect up to 35,000 ants and termites a day. They do this by using their 60-centimetre-long, very sticky tongues to lick up as many insects as possible. One of the reasons their tongues are so effective at this is because they are covered with tiny backward-facing barbs that trap the ants.

They also have a large, bushy tail which can sometimes make it hard to tell which end is the head and which is the tail. They use this tail as a blanket in the colder months and to give them shade in the hotter months.

Conservation Status

VULNERABLE

The anteater has survived for 25 million years on earth, yet in the last 10 years it has started to disappear at a rapid rate through land loss, poaching and road accidents.

In areas like Brazil, the giant anteater is caught and killed for its supposed medicinal uses, as well as for food and leather products. Unfortunately, it is suspected there are only about 5,000 left in the wild.

Close Relations

The anteater, armadillo and sloth are all part of a group of mammals called *Xenarthra*. There are some key identifying features which remain the same between these groups: for example, they all have razor-sharp claws.

Diet

Since they must eat such an enormous quantity of ants and termites every day to ensure they have enough energy, giant anteaters have evolved the ability to move their tongues as fast as 160 times a minute. They conserve energy by keeping their other movements slow.

Although they can eat many species of ants, giant anteaters have learned which species sting the most and will steer clear of those mounds.

Location/Habitat

Giant anteaters are now extinct in Guatemala and Belize but can be found in other parts of Central and South America, such as Argentina, Paraguay and Bolivia. They enjoy a variety of habitats but are usually found in grasslands, forests and plantations.

Fun Facts

→ Baby anteaters ride on their mothers' backs, which makes the mother look larger and more threatening.

→ Despite their prehistoric appearance, giant anteaters only live as long as a typical dog – around 14 years.

→ Their claws are generally used to tear holes in termite and ant mounds but can be used in self-defence and to protect their young against predators. They have even been known to kill jaguars!

Goblin Shark

Mitsukurina owstoni

(mit-soo-kur-e-na o-stone-e)

Description

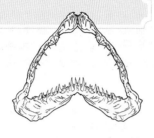

The goblin shark spends most of its time deep in the ocean and is very rarely seen by other animals, or even by other goblin sharks. It's definitely not the most attractive sea creature to come across, but there's a good reason behind its ugly appearance.

Goblin sharks grow to around 3.9 metres long and, when their jaws are retracted, look similar to any other species of shark, except for their pinkish-purple colouring. Unlike other sharks, they have flexible jaws and can very quickly turn their mouths, crammed full of menacing teeth, outward to snap up passing food. This doesn't just make them look unique, it helps them catch prey without having to exert energy by propelling their whole body forward. Such a large, deep-sea animal needs to conserve energy as much as possible, so this adaptation is very useful.

Conservation Status

LEAST CONCERN

Little is known about these deep-water sharks. However, it is thought there are very few threats to their survival, other than being caught as bycatch by deep-sea trawlers, which are detrimental to sea-floor habitats.

Diet

With their powerful mouths, they feed on squid, fish, crabs and crustaceans. Because there is so little light deep in the ocean, goblin sharks, like other deep-sea animals, do not have much need for strong eyesight. Instead, they rely on their snout, which is full of electroreceptors, to burrow through the seabed and sense where potential prey may be hiding.

Location/Habitat

It is thought goblin sharks live mostly in the waters around Japan, because this is where most recorded sightings have been. However, there have also been sightings throughout the Atlantic, Pacific and Indian Oceans, and even a few spotted off the coasts of New South Wales and Tasmania in Australia. To find them yourself, you must be at depths between 40 and 1,300 metres, hanging out near the seabed.

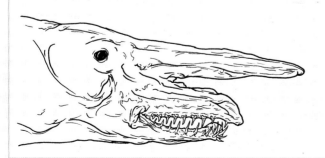

Fun Facts

→ Goblin shark jaws and teeth are highly sought after within the trade industry, and can be sold for up to $5,000.

→ These sharks have not been studied in their natural habitat because they live in such deep waters.

→ Fewer than 50 specimens have been found in the last 118 years.

→ Their jaws can open 111 degrees, whereas humans can only reach around 50 degrees.

→ When they are fully extended, their jaws can be up to 9.4% of their total body length.

Mitsukurina owstoni

Centrocercus urophasianus

Greater Sage Grouse

Centrocercus urophasianus
(cent-ro-ser-cus yuro-fas-e-ar-nus)

Description

Greater sage grouse can reach up to 60 centimetres tall and weigh up to around 3 kilograms. The females and males look very different, with the females appearing quite plain in comparison. The male sage grouse has two rather grand chest accessories, which they can fill with around a gallon of air by breathing in. These large, egg-shaped balloons sound just as ridiculous as they look. When filled, they can be shaken to make wobbly, popping sounds. The purpose of these unusual lumps is to attract a mate during breeding season. In order to secure a mate, male sage grouse will also show off by fanning their magnificent tail feathers.

Conservation Status

NEAR THREATENED

Due to the increasing demand for crops such as wheat and potatoes, as well as products like oil and gas, the habitats of the sage grouse are fast being cleared, causing a reduction in their population. Sage grouse are very sensitive to human disruption and the number of sage grouse present is an indication of how healthy the ecosystem is. Unfortunately, areas that used to be home to sage grouse are now so widely used by humans that the birds inhabit only half their original range.

Diet

These birds are herbivores and spend their days feeding on fresh shoots and leaves. In warmer months, they can also be found eating small insects and flowers. The best habitats will have water sources close by, but where this is not possible, the grouse will fly up to 5 kilometres twice a day for a drink.

Location/Habitat

As their name suggests, the sage grouse is found in sagebrush plains. These are located in western United States and in south-eastern Canada. Between March and May, sage grouse will visit the courting grounds known as 'leks' to complete their mating displays.

Fun Facts

→ The typical lifespan for a sage grouse is 3–6 years but females usually live longer than males as males are more sought after for their luxurious feathers.

→ During the winter months, they will obtain their water by eating snow.

→ Although there can be 70 or so males present during mating displays, generally only one or two will be chosen by the females to mate with.

→ Males will stand beside females during their courtship dance. This is because their air sacs produce the loudest noises when heard from the side.

→ Chicks are almost completely self-sufficient soon after birth, which is very impressive because they are incubated for only three weeks!

Hairless Chinese Crested Dog

Canis lupus familiaris
(kay-nis loo-pus fam-ili-aris)

Description

There are actually two different types of Chinese crested dog: the hairless and the powder puff. The hairless is definitely the more unfortunate looking of the two, with hair growing only on parts of its face, feet and tail. There is an established link between hairless breeds of dog and poor teeth longevity, so the hairless Chinese crested dog often has odd gappy teeth.

These dogs typically weigh only 4.5 kilograms and grow to 33 centimetres long.

Conservation Status

NOT EVALUATED

The Chinese crested dog comes under the scientific category of domesticated dogs, so they do not have their own evaluation. However, records going as far back as the late 1800s suggest their numbers are abundant.

Diet

Like most domesticated dogs, this breed will feed on a range of pre-packaged dog foods, rather than going out and hunting for themselves.

Location/Habitat

This breed of dog is thought to have become common in North America around 1974, having been bred from Mexican and African hairless dogs. They do not actually originate from China as their name would suggest, and can now be found all over the world.

Since these animals are small, they do not require a lot of exercise and are happy to live in small houses or apartments.

Fun Facts

→ Hairless Chinese crested dogs can live to approximately 12 years of age.

→ Because they have no hair on most of their bodies, they can be prone to skin conditions. Getting blackheads is one of them!

→ It is thought that in the 1500s, the predecessors to Chinese crested dogs were used on ships to help rid the vessels of rats and mice, which were potential carriers of the plague.

→ Their predecessors were also used by Aztecs as portable heaters in colder climates.

→ They are one of the most popular breeds to enter the World's Ugliest Dog Contest and often take home the prize.

Canis lupus familiaris

Hypsignathus monstrosus

Hammer-headed Fruit Bat

Hypsignathus monstrosus
(hip-sig-nay-thus mon-stro-sus)

Description

The male hammer-headed fruit bat features a shockingly large nose and drooping lips. The purpose of their enormous snout is to generate loud honking sounds that help them attract females. Size and weight vary between the sexes, with the females averaging 21 centimetres and 275 grams, while the males average 25 centimetres and 377 grams.

Diet

Figs, guavas, bananas and mangos make up most of the hammer-headed fruit bat's diet. Males have been known to travel up to 10 kilometres in search of the best fruit.

Conservation Status

LEAST CONCERN

This species is occasionally hunted and eaten, but its most immediate threat is the destruction of its habitat for logging. These bats can also be infected by deadly parasites.

Location/Habitat

You can find hammer-headed fruit bats on the equator in West and Central Africa. They perch in trees, surrounded by mangrove swamps, rivers and palm forests in groups of around five.

Close Relations

The hammer-headed fruit bat is closely related to the fruit bat, *Pteropodidae*.

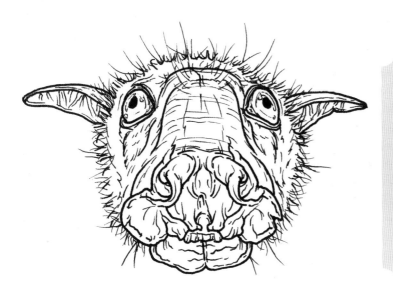

Fun Facts

> Hammer-headed fruit bats have a 30-year life expectancy in the wild.

> A group of hammer-headed fruit bats is called a cloud.

> They have a wing span of nearly 1 metre.

> In rare cases, the hammer-headed bat has been known to attack chickens, hunting them for meat and drinking their blood.

Hellbender

Cryptobranchus alleganiensis
(crip-toe-brank-us al-eg-ani-en-sis)

Description

Hellbenders' prehistoric appearance makes a lot of sense given they have been found to have existed all the way back to 160 million years ago! They are thought to be the third-largest salamander and can reach lengths of 74 centimetres for females and 68.6 centimetres for males. Most are around 20–30 centimetres shorter than this though, and weigh anywhere between 405 and 1,010 grams.

They are slimy, an adaptation which helps them move smoothly over rocky or muddy floors. It also helps protect them from predators. Hellbenders secrete a form of mucus/goo from their skin which irritates anything that comes too close. It is also the origin of their nickname, 'snot otters'.

Conservation Status

NEAR THREATENED

These disturbing-looking creatures are facing a number of serious threats including the loss of their habitat and pollution. Because their nesting sites and habitats are found at the base of rocky environments, they are easily covered or destroyed through mining, logging and other human-caused land loss. Hellbenders are even threatened by superstition and mass collection. Many fishermen believe they are deadly and will kill them on sight, and their popularity as pets and in the collection trade means their numbers in the wild are dwindling.

Diet

A strange thing about hellbenders is that they have been found to ingest their own eggs during mating season. Fortunately, they don't eat all of them – they leave most to grow and hatch. Aside from this snack, they largely feed on crayfish and the occasional fish, insect, tadpole or smaller salamander. By investigating captured specimens, scientists have discovered that hellbenders are bottom feeders. Scientists know this because the hellbenders' stomachs contained materials from the floor of their habitat – mud and rocks, for example.

Location/Habitat

The hellbender is a freshwater creature which you can find living 15–60 centimetres below the surface of streams, rivers and creeks in chillier temperatures around the United States. They can be tricky to see because they like to rest during the day and hunt at night, and because they like rocky and muddy areas with plenty of large sticks and logs to hide beneath.

Fun Facts

→ Hellbenders can live to 30 years old, however they usually only reach half that age due to over-capturing, pollution and habitat destruction.

→ Up to 450 eggs can be laid during just one month a year, usually September to October.

→ The meaning behind their strange name is not entirely known. It is thought it might refer to an early description of them as looking 'like they crawled out of hell and are bent on going back'.

→ Hellbenders have been known to swallow fish nearly as large as they are.

Cryptobranchus alleganiensis

Numida meleagris

Helmeted Guineafowl

Numida meleagris
(nu-me-da mel-e-a-gris)

Description

Although the helmeted guineafowl's feathers are generally thought to be quite beautiful, their wrinkly, featherless heads are considered rather ugly. Like the southern cassowaries on page 111, they have dangling wattles. These are more vibrant in the males, probably to attract a mate. They also have a horn similar to that of the southern cassowary, although the use of the helmeted guineafowl's is unknown.

They are extremely vocal birds, whether it be during mating displays or when feeling threatened, and many farmers who own these guineafowls have noticed they make great replacements for guard dogs, as they call out in response to intruding animals or humans.

Conservation Status

LEAST CONCERN

Helmeted guineafowl numbers are stable because they are farmed for their eggs, meat and attractive feathers, and are also kept as pets. Due to their skittish nature and small size, they have many predators, such as wild dogs, cats and large snakes.

Diet

One reason helmeted guineafowl are so popular as pets is their tendency to eat small snakes, ticks and rodents, whether it be out of curiosity or hunger. They also eat seeds, berries and plants.

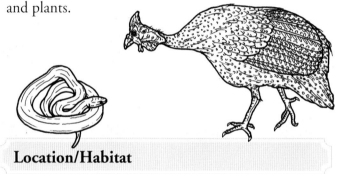

Location/Habitat

In the wild, these guineafowl can be found in a variety of habitats such as bush, forests, grasslands or even deserts on rare occasions! It all depends on where they find themselves scratching around for food.

They are native to many regions of Africa but due to their growing popularity as pets and money makers, they can now be found all over the world.

Fun Facts

→ The collective noun for guineafowl is a confusion.

→ They were originally domesticated for food purposes by the ancient Romans.

→ They can grow to be 15 years old.

→ The horn on their heads, otherwise known as a casque, is made from the same materials as your fingernails and toenails – keratin.

Rhinoplax vigil

Helmeted Hornbill

Rhinoplax vigil
(ryno-plax vig-il)

Description

These enormous, striking birds are one of the largest species of hornbills and can reach 120 centimetres tall, excluding their tail feathers. These feathers can reach 50 centimetres on their own.

Their horns are around 30 centimetres long on average and weigh in at around 3 kilograms for males and 2.7 kilograms for females. They actually account for 10% of the birds' total body weight.

Helmeted hornbills use these horns, otherwise known as casques, in fights with other hornbills when defending their mates, eggs and territory. This species is sexually dimorphic, meaning that the male and female have different appearances. The females have a pale blue wrinkled neck pouch, whereas the males' is deep burgundy.

Conservation Status

CRITICALLY ENDANGERED

Unfortunately, because of excessive hunting and land clearing for logging and palm oil plantations, it is thought this irreplaceable species will become extinct in the near future.

In 2013, as many as 6,000 birds were killed for trade purposes alone in West Kalimantan in Borneo. Helmeted hornbills have unique 'red ivory' horns which are used to make jewellery and ornaments and can be sold for large sums.

Although hunting the helmeted hornbill has been illegal for years, and is punishable by up to five years in prison, these amazing birds are still killed and traded. Enforced laws and rehabilitation projects are urgently needed to save this species from extinction.

Diet

Despite their fierce-looking beaks, these hornbills feast predominately on fruit. This makes them fantastic seed dispersers, as the seeds are not broken down through digestion and are distributed around the forest through the birds' droppings.

They have also been spotted eating other small animals, like snakes and insects, and even other larger birds such as fellow hornbills!

Location/Habitat

These birds are native to Indonesia, Malaysia, Thailand, Borneo, Myanmar, Sumatra and Brunei. They live up high in the trees of lowland, semi-evergreen or evergreen forests. It is important the trees have high branches for the males to keep watch from, and also suitable nesting nooks for the females.

Fun Facts

→ They are the only species of hornbill, out of 60, to have non-hollow casques. Theirs are made entirely of bone and fused to their skull.

→ The Bornean Dayak tribe sees these birds as messengers of the gods and so it is forbidden to kill them.

→ Mating couples seal their nesting hollows with their own poo to protect the female and her babies.

→ When fighting, helmeted hornbills have been seen to fly directly into one another and clash heads, a sound which can be heard over 100 metres away.

→ If they eat too many fermented figs, they can become drunk.

Humpback Anglerfish

Melanocetus johnsonii

(melon-o-see-tus john-sony-eye)

Description

These disturbing-looking fish appear the way they do for good reason – their ugly appearance helps them feed and protect themselves at great depths.

Since no light is able to penetrate as deep in the ocean as these fish live, they have evolved their own source of light, known as an 'esca' or 'illicium', which acts as a lure to attract prey and draw them in close enough for the anglerfish to snap up. This light is called bioluminescence and is created by the fish's symbiotic bacteria.

In this species, the females are approximately five times larger than the males and are also more dominant. Females can reach up to 15.4 centimetres long, whereas males only grow to 2.8 centimetres – a very extreme case of sexual dimorphism!

Conservation Status

LEAST CONCERN

Despite living so far from human populations, deep-sea humpback anglerfish still face threats caused by humans. These include the possibility of being caught as by-catch in trawlers as well as shifting water conditions due to climate change.

Diet

Because of their esca, or lure, these fish do not need to be speedy swimmers – hence their round body shape. Instead, they drift slowly through the water, waiting for prey to come to them. They eat animals such as other fish, jellyfish and krill, and can use their sharp, angled teeth and large mouths to capture and eat prey twice their size.

Location/Habitat

The humpback anglerfish lives in the Indian, Atlantic and Pacific Oceans. However, you will not come across one of these creatures, as they live deep down in the mesopelagic and bathypelagic zones of the ocean – in cold, dark depths of up to 2,100 metres.

Fun Facts

→ They are also known as humpback blackdevils.

→ There have only been eight male specimens recorded, in comparison to 852 females.

→ It is a common occurrence in other anglerfish for males to latch on to females and become parasitic, sucking their blood. Luckily for humpback anglerfish females, this is not the case for this species, with males only visiting the females for mating purposes.

→ These fish have tiny eyes in comparison to their bodies, which makes sense because they live in the darkness and have very little use for eyes.

→ The males have only one goal in life: search for a mate, latch on, fertilise the egg, then leave to find another partner.

Melanocetus johnsonii

Sarcoramphus papa

King Vulture

Sarcoramphus papa

(sark-o-ram-fus pa-pa)

Description

Unlike other species of vulture, the king vulture does not have long, luscious eyelashes. They make up for this, however, with the vivid and colourful patterning on their faces.

These vultures can have a wingspan of almost 2 metres and grow to 81 centimetres from head to tail. They usually weigh up to 4.5 kilograms.

They are a sexually monomorphic bird, which means both sexes look the same. Each has white feathers and a colourful face. Like other vultures, they have a bald head, which is thought to prevent them from getting too dirty when feeding on their messy meals of rotting flesh. This helps prevent the spread of diseases.

Conservation Status

LEAST CONCERN

Although the king vulture is thought to be of least concern in terms of conservation, it is believed there are only around 50,000 individual birds alive today.

This may seem like a lot, but the number is declining due to habitat destruction through logging and deforestation.

Their numbers are also impacted negatively by snakes who prey on their eggs and by large mammals who can attack them when they are in vulnerable positions.

Close Relations

They are closely related to the turkey vulture, featured on page 120.

Diet

These birds are scavengers, meaning they do not kill their food themselves but instead eat roadkill, leftovers from other predators or animals that have died from natural causes. Although this process may seem unhygienic and gross, it is actually extremely beneficial for the environment, as it prevents the spread of pathogens and cleans up the earth.

Location/Habitat

King vultures live in Argentina, Mexico and other regions of Central and South America and will remain in the same area all year round. They reside in the highest part of the trees, which makes spotting them rather difficult. They enjoy forest-like environments and lay their eggs in logs and stump hollows.

Fun Facts

→ King vultures can live up to 30 years!

→ The collective noun for a group of king vultures is a solitary.

→ It is thought they make their nesting sites extra stinky in order to discourage predators from looking too closely.

→ They are at their most vulnerable when feeding because they cannot take flight easily with a full stomach. They will often vomit up their food to make themselves light enough for take-off.

→ The name 'king vulture' is thought to refer to the Mayan legend in which this species was the 'king' who transferred the messages between the gods and humans.

Largetooth Sawfish

Pristis pristis
(pris-tis pris-tis)

Description

Largetooth sawfish can grow to massive lengths of over 6.5 metres from tip to tail, and can weigh as much as 600 kilograms! They get their name from what appear to be teeth along their saw-like rostrums, but in fact these sharp growths are actually scales. Instead of using their unusual adaptation like a knife, they use it to locate and stun their food in muddy riverbeds.

Another useful adaptation they have evolved is that their mouths are on the underside of their face, in the perfect position to suction up fast-moving prey beneath them.

Conservation Status

CRITICALLY ENDANGERED

The full population of the largetooth sawfish is not known because there are very few reports about them and they are often confused for other fish. However, it is thought that they have already become extinct in many of the areas they once inhabited. This is due both to being accidentally caught in fishing nets and to direct fishing. Largetooth sawfish are hunted for their body parts, such as their unique rostra or their skin, which is turned into leather for clothing.

Around 1,000–2,000 snouts are sold in the Brazilian fish markets every year. The teeth-like scales on their rostrums are often used as decorative elements on weaponry or as ingredients in soups.

Diet

With a snout like theirs, you would expect largetooth sawfish to be a vicious threat to most sea creatures, but these sawfish prefer to feed on small invertebrates, schools of fish and crustaceans.

Location/Habitat

While their full range is unknown, largetooth sawfish have been recorded living in the waters of southeast Asia, New Guinea and the western Indian Ocean. They can also be found in large numbers living on the coast of northern Australia, which is an area that has protection measures in place to assist with conservation.

As their body is long and flat, they like to lay low on riverbeds in muddy environments which help them camouflage. They can be found in fresh waters such as rivers and estuaries and prefer to spend time at depths of around 10 metres.

Fun Facts

→ Although they prefer fresh water, largetooth sawfish are euryhaline, which means they can survive in both fresh- and saltwater habitats.

→ It is estimated that the oldest recorded largetooth sawfish was 35 years old.

→ Babies are not hatched from an egg laid on the riverbed like many other underwater species. Instead, the eggs are incubated inside the mother until they are ready to emerge as functioning sawfish.

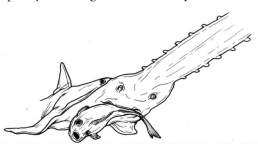

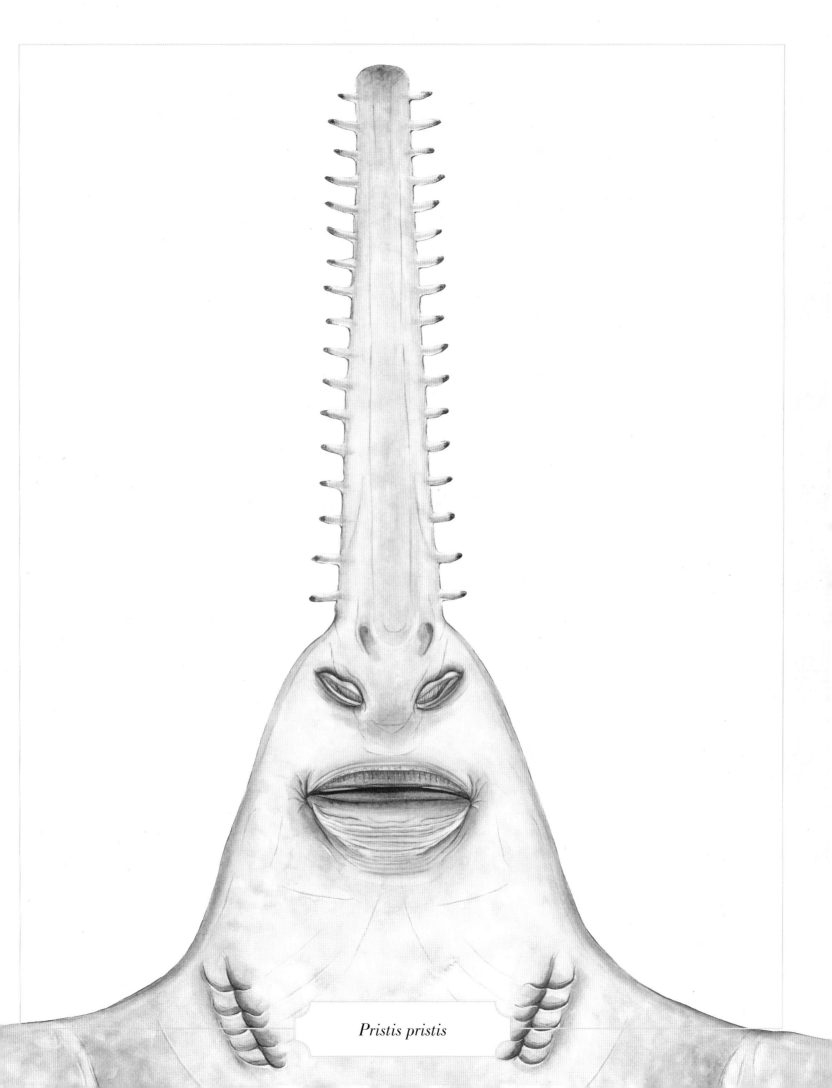

Pristis pristis

Tapirus indicus

Malayan Tapir

Tapirus indicus
(tay-peer-us in-deek-us)

Description

The Malayan tapir's long, trunk-like nose, no matter how disproportionate it may seem, is very useful when feeding and especially when swimming, since it acts as a built-in snorkel. Their black and white colouration also has a purpose. Because they are nocturnal (meaning they are most active at night), being black and white helps them blend into the tree trunks. To predators, the black parts blend in with the trees, and the white looks like the space between them.

Being the largest species of tapir in the world, they weigh an average of 275 kilograms, but can reach as much 540 kilograms and develop to lengths of 2.5 metres.

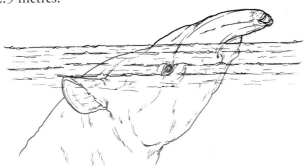

Conservation Status

ENDANGERED

Although hunting tapirs is illegal, it is still a significant cause of their diminishing numbers.

However, the leading cause of their endangered status is habitat loss as land is cleared to make room for palm oil plantations or other industries. Because other species numbers are also declining due to deforestation, tapirs are being targeted by new predators who can't find enough of their usual food source.

Close Relations

The closest relatives to the tapir are the common horse and also the rhinoceros. A feature rhinos and tapirs have in common is their uneven number of toes. They both have three toes on their back feet.

Diet

The Malayan tapir can be found feeding on grass and the leaves, fruits and flowers of small trees.

Location/Habitat

They are native to parts of Malaysia, Indonesia, Thailand and Myanmar, and since they love to wallow in pools of water to cool down, they can be found in lowland habitats, moving to hilly forests for the rainy seasons. They usually live alone, though mothers and their young will live together for up to eight months.

Fun Facts

→ The collective noun for a group of these tapirs is a candle.

→ They have the longest snout of all tapir species.

→ If you find yourself near a tapir, make sure to stand far away because they are known for spraying their urine long distances in territorial displays.

→ Tapirs love to poo in water.

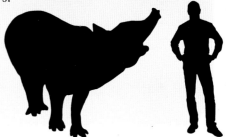

Maleo

Macrocephalon maleo
(macro-sef-a-lon mal-e-o)

Description

While it may look like the result of a painful bump, the bony horn on the maleo's head is actually a casque, similar to that of the helmeted hornbills and cassowaries found on pages 65 and 111. The purpose of the maleo's casque is not fully understood, since both males and females have one and so it is unlikely to be related to sexual attraction.

Standing at around 60 centimetres tall, these shy birds remain quiet unless around their nesting grounds or if they feel threatened. They take turns to stand guard over their nests and watch for predators.

Conservation Status

ENDANGERED

One of the leading factors contributing to falling maleo numbers is the introduction of egg harvesting. Another major contributor has been the destruction of their habitats through deforestation and commercial logging. This has also resulted in the introduction of invasive species like dogs and rats, which feed on the maleo and their chicks. These factors have caused the maleo population to decline by 90% in the last half-century.

Diet

Like other birds of the Sulawesi region in Indonesia, maleos spend their days feeding on a range of seeds, roots and fruits, as well as small invertebrates such as insects.

Location/Habitat

The maleo is endemic – which means it's native to or found only in – the Buton Islands and Sulawesi, Indonesia. They like to nest communally because having more birds around provides more protection against predators. Maleos nest in riverbanks and sandy floors as this is the ideal environment to hatch their eggs. They dig pits into the ground and lay their large eggs before covering them with sand. The birds rely on solar heat to maintain the nest at a warm temperature for two to three months. If the temperature of the sand drops or rises too drastically, the chicks will not survive.

Fun Facts

→ When maleos reach adolescence, they find the partner they will stay with for life.

→ Maleo eggs are enormous in comparison to their bodies and can be around five times the size of a chicken egg.

→ Because their eggs are so big in comparison to the birds, females will often faint from exhaustion while laying them.

→ Their eggs hatch underground, so chicks can take up to two days to dig to the surface and begin their lives.

Macrocephalon maleo

Mandrillus sphinx

Mandrill

Mandrillus sphinx
(man-drill-us sphinks)

Description

It is impossible to look past the mandrill's brilliant colours, which are found on both their faces and their bottoms. This colouration is an evolutionary adaptation that helps these primates express their emotions. A great example of this is that the patches of colour on their rump, chest, wrists and ankles will grow brighter to signify excitement, submissiveness, or to show that they are ready to mate.

Another way in which they communicate is through opening their mouths, which lets other mandrills know they are happy and feeling friendly. A larger, more open mouth, known as 'yawning', shows off their 4.5-centimetre-long teeth and lets potential threats know they are angry.

Males and females of this species look different. Males can grow up to 90 centimetres tall, and weigh 50 kilograms, whereas the females are significantly smaller. Females are also much less colourful than the males.

Conservation Status

VULNERABLE

Due to the mandrill's loud and distinctive calls, they are easily targeted by hunters and often killed for their prized meat. This, paired with the destruction of their habitats through logging and deforestation, has caused their numbers to decline by over 30% since the 1990s. These incredible animals now require human protection to stop their falling numbers.

Diet

Mandrills eat a variety of plants, as well as small invertebrates and vertebrates. Their diet consists of things like roots, flowers, leaves, snails, worms, snakes and lizards.

Location/Habitat

Mandrills are terrestrial, meaning they spend most of their time on the ground, and live in the forests and thick scrub of west Africa, in areas around the Congo River, western Gabon and Equatorial Guinea. Mandrills will climb into trees to sleep overnight as this helps keep them safe from predators.

A group of these primates can be as large as 50 individuals, and there is usually only one male whose job it is to protect the group from danger and mate with the females.

Fun Facts

- Mandrills will ferociously hit the ground to display their anger.
- The females of the group will help to raise young that is not theirs.
- They have been recorded to live to 46 years of age.
- Like humans, these primates have opposable thumbs, which help them to grip branches and to climb.
- The collective noun for a group of mandrills is a barrel or a wilderness.

Marabou Stork

Leptoptilos crumeniferus
(lep-top-til-os crew-men-ifer-us)

Description

Once fully grown, these bald birds can reach
1.5 metres tall, with a wing span of 2.6 metres.
Beneath their beaks – which can grow up to
26 centimetres long – the male storks have a huge
pink sack that is connected to their nostrils. During
mating displays, the stork breathes into this sac to
expand it and makes a croaking sound to entice
potential mates.

Unlike other birds, marabou storks mate for life.
Both the male and female bird help feed and protect
their young.

Conservation Status

LEAST CONCERN

The marabou stork's ugly appearance doesn't protect
it from being hunted and sold at markets across
Africa for its feathers and meat. Despite this, the
stork population continues to grow because of the
increasing number of landfills throughout Africa,
which provide this resilient stork with an endless
supply of food.

Close Relations

The marabou stork is a member
of the same family as the turkey
vulture, *Cathartes aura*, on page 120.

Diet

Marabou storks are scavenger birds, meaning they
feed on animals that are already dead. They play
an important part in the ecosystem by cleaning up
decaying leftovers from water sources and preventing
the spread of germs. Occasionally, they will kill
other animals to eat, such as small mammals, birds
and insects.

Location/Habitat

Found south of the Sahara Desert in Africa, these
unique creatures dwell in open, aquatic areas such
as along river edges and in swamps. They sometimes
live close to humans, for example in garbage dumps
or near meat facilities. Marabou storks build their
nests out of sticks and twigs, way up high in
the treetops.

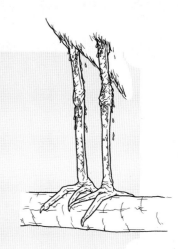

Fun Facts

> Like all birds, marabou storks' long legs are made from hollow bones,
which have evolved for flying.

> They can live to the ripe old age of 25 in the wild.

> They are known as the 'undertaker bird' because they look like traditional grave
diggers, with a black suit and coat tails.

> They deliberately poo on themselves and allow the poo to run down their legs
because it acts as a disinfectant and cools them down.

Leptoptilos crumeniferus

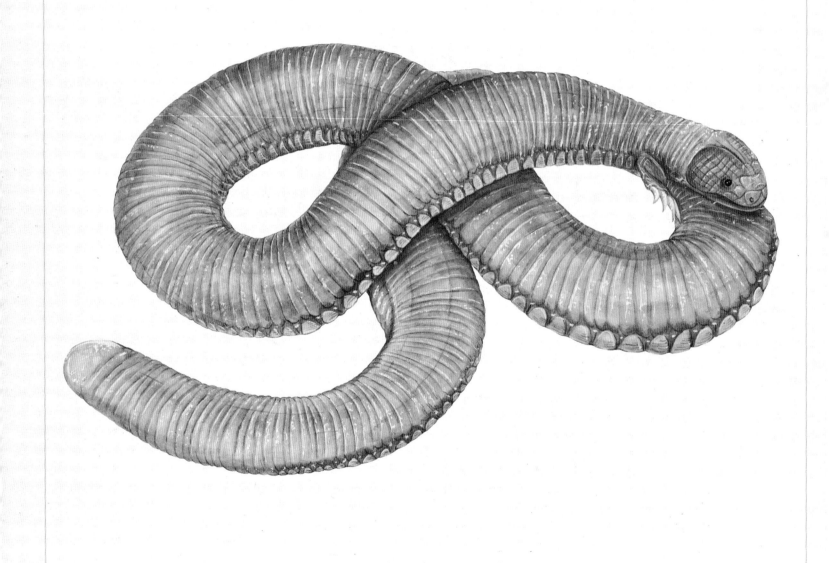

Bipes biporus

Mexican Mole Lizard

Bipes biporus
(byeps bye-poor-us)

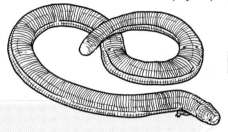

Description

These pinkish lizards are sexually monomorphic and look the same whether they are male or female. There is, however, a difference between the adults and young. As these lizards grow older, they not only grow longer (reaching up to 19 centimetres) but also fade to a paler shade. There is also a higher chance that older lizards will be missing their tails! These lizards have evolved the ability to detach their own tail when chased by a predator, leaving it behind to distract the hunter while the lizard flees.

The mole lizard's body, front limbs and claws are well adapted to travelling and digging through tight burrows and it can even adjust its body temperature according to the soil.

Diet

The Mexican mole lizard eats a huge number of mites, ants, termites, cockroaches and other small animals, proving to be a great form of pest control for nearby humans. Despite their size, they will attempt to eat almost any animal that will fit into their mouths.

Location/Habitat

It is quite tricky to find these animals in their natural habitats as they spend most of their time underground in their tunnel systems, avoiding almost all threats and predators. However, if you do want to go searching, you will need to travel to the Baja California Peninsula of Mexico.

Conservation Status

LEAST CONCERN

This unpleasant-looking creature is sometimes killed by local people who mistake it for a snake. However, this unique animal poses no threat to humans and is actually as harmless as a large earthworm. Despite occasionally being killed by humans, the Mexican mole lizard faces minimal threats to its range and population and is therefore considered of least concern in terms of conservation.

Fun Facts

- Unfortunately, Mexican mole lizards cannot regrow their tail, so they must use their detachment strategy wisely.
- Although they look like snakes, they are more closely related to lizards.
- The oldest recorded Mexican mole lizard was three years old.
- This species of mole lizard is one of only three out of 200 that have legs.
- Aside from humans, their other predators are mammals such as skunks who sometimes come across the lizards while digging around.

Monkey Slug Caterpillar

Phobetron pithecium
(fobe-tron pith-e-see-um)

Description

Unlike many other species of caterpillar, monkey slugs have no legs! Instead they use their fleshy bodies, with suction cups on the base, to slide themselves across the ground.

These caterpillars can reach lengths of 2.5 centimetres and have a furry, brown texture which gives them their name. What their name doesn't allude to is that they have six leg-like limbs that grow out of their upper bodies. These do not act like real limbs but are an adaptation to protect against predators. While they look to be covered in soft fur, these appendages are actually covered in tiny, sharp hairs which are extremely painful to anyone who touches them. These growths fall off before adulthood.

Conservation Status

NOT EVALUATED

Like *Creatonotos gangis*, monkey slug caterpillars are somewhat of a mystery. Very little is known about them and their conservation status has not been evaluated. Hopefully, more research will be done in the future so we can understand their population and the threats to it.

Diet

Not much is known about the monkey slug caterpillar's diet, however it is thought they eat the leaves of bushes and trees such as oaks.

Once they have transformed into moths, it is believed their diet consists of a variety of liquids such as sap, fruit juice and flower nectar, sucked up through their straw-like tongue, otherwise known as a proboscis.

Location/Habitat

It is thought these caterpillars, and the moths they turn into, live on the eastern side of the United States, wherever their favourite trees are found. These trees include willows, apples, chestnuts, oaks and many others.

Fun Facts

→ The monkey slug caterpillar grows into the hag moth. Both are as unfortunate in appearance as their names suggest.

→ Because of their threatening nature, they are thought to ward off other small predators, with only other monkey slugs being brave enough to face them.

→ The males and females both appear very similar, which is known as monomorphism.

→ When they create their cocoon, they put their bizarre limb-like growths on the outside to ward off predators.

→ Because of their suction cups, they can only move very slowly.

Phobetron pithecium

Heterocephalus glaber

Naked Mole Rat

Heterocephalus glaber
(het-e-ro-sef-a-lus glar-ber)

Description

The reason these rats look rather strange is because they have developed some impressive adaptations to slow their aging process and to decrease pain receptors. Although they are 'naked' they have no sensitivity in their skin, so they don't feel pain.

Naked mole rats have evolved over time so that their teeth are on the outside of their mouths, which allows them to dig without swallowing dirt. Their loose skin helps them pass each other in the narrow tunnels without getting stuck.

Most of a colony's rats are workers, who average up to 7.5 centimetres long and weigh around 30 grams. There is only one queen rat whose role it is to run the colony and give birth to new young, and she can weigh as much as 71 grams.

Conservation Status

LEAST CONCERN

The naked mole rat has a relatively large distribution area, helping ensure a sustainable population. Their numbers seem to be growing. Their habitats are essentially untouched since they spend their days and nights underground in tunnels. However, since they use their burrows to find root vegetables under the ground, they have the potential to be treated as pests by farmers if their numbers increase too dramatically.

Diet

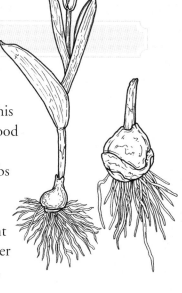

Naked mole rats live almost entirely underground and very rarely visit the surface. This means they must survive on food that is found underneath the earth, such as roots, plant bulbs and stems (otherwise known as tubers). These are collected by the worker rats and brought back to the colony for the other rats and the queen to feast on.

Location/Habitat

These wrinkly rats can be found in eastern Africa, in areas like central Ethiopia, Somalia, Kenya and Djibouti, but they will not be seen unless in a zoo or if you happen to live underground too. They rely on complex tunnels which can be found 2 metres below the surface and can reach up to 4 kilometres long.

Fun Facts

→ Naked mole rats can survive without air for up to 18 minutes.

→ They can run just as fast backward as they can forward.

→ They have been documented to live to 30 years old. This species holds the record for the longest-living rodent.

→ They do not need to drink water as their diet provides enough to keep them hydrated.

→ To absorb as many nutrients as possible from a single meal, the rats will often eat each other's poo.

North Sulawesi Babirusa

Babyrousa celebensis
(baby-roo-sa seleb-en-sis)

Description

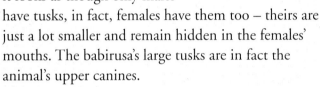

This 60–100 kilogram mammal stands out not just for its size and tusks, but also because of its hairless, wrinkly skin, which is unique to this species of babirusa. Although it looks as though only males have tusks, in fact, females have them too – theirs are just a lot smaller and remain hidden in the females' mouths. The babirusa's large tusks are in fact the animal's upper canines.

It is likely that males grow these large tusks for display rather than for combat. The tusks are too thin and brittle to withstand much force and so when males fight, they stand on their hind legs and 'box' each other rather than use their tusks.

Their tusks grow throughout their lives and can reach 43 centimetres long. Sometimes they get out of control and, in rare instances, can grow through a babirusa's skull.

Conservation Status

VULNERABLE

Unfortunately, due to the size and hunting popularity of the Sulawesi babirusa, they are usually the first species to disappear from the ecosystem when logging and deforestation take place. As their habitats are destroyed, they become much easier to spot and can be easily hunted for their meat and teeth or tusks. Reports show that their numbers have dropped by 30% in the last 20 years, with another 10% drop expected in the near future.

Diet

Looking at the fierce tusks of the babirusa, you would expect it to eat something large and frightening. This is not the case. Babirusas forage through the sand and mud for leaves, fruits, roots, insects, fish and small animals and use their powerful jaws to crack nuts.

Location/Habitat

Like their name suggests, they are found primarily in Sulawesi, Indonesia. Sadly, because of heavy hunting, it is difficult to find the exact distribution of this species. Previously, they enjoyed living in low-lying areas around riverbanks and rainforests, where there was a huge number of different food sources. Due to the increased number of threats brought on by habitat destruction, they have moved to higher ground which, being harder to get to, is safer for them.

Fun Facts

→ Like dogs, babirusas will sometimes act excited and playful when seeing familiar faces that they associate with food or fun. They will even wag their tail and jump around.

→ They live to around 24 years old.

→ Did you wonder what the name 'babirusa' meant? It is a Malay term meaning 'pig deer'.

→ Their haunting appearance is often the inspiration behind masks made by locals, who have also been known to gift babirusas to visiting guests.

→ Although they may look a lot like common pigs, it is thought the two species branched from a common ancestor very early on in their evolution.

Babyrousa celebensis

Geronticus eremita

Northern Bald Ibis

Geronticus eremita
(jer-on-tik-us erem-ita)

Description

As pointed out in their name, these birds are considered ugly because of their featherless heads, which are often pink and grey in colour.

Their comical appearance is believed to result from either an adaptation to prevent dirtying their heads when eating or one intended to attract a mate. Their bodies are covered in iridescent feathers and they can grow to 70–80 centimetres in length and weigh around 1.2 kilograms.

Conservation Status

CRITICALLY ENDANGERED

Trophy hunting and encroaching human infrastructure have drastically reduced the numbers of the already small population of northern bald ibis.

Recently in Turkey there was a mass death of these birds caused by second-hand poisoning from pesticides used to control the mosquitoes and locusts in the area.

Close Relations

The northern bald ibis is closely related to the commonly seen Australian white ibis, *Threskiornis moluccus*, which is sometimes called the 'bin chicken'.

The family resemblance is clear in the similar body and beak shape.

Diet

This species of ibis feeds on a range of plants, berries and roots, as well as small animals such as worms, snakes, insects, fish and amphibians. They even occasionally feast on rodents and other birds.

Location/Habitat

The northern bald ibis was originally native to the Middle East, central Europe and north Africa but now, due to a massive decline in numbers, they are only found in Turkey, Syria and Morocco.

Their habitat varies from natural, such as wetlands, fields, trees, cliff edges, to man-made, such as walls and old castles.

Fun Facts
* These ibis live for a relatively long time for birds, sometimes getting to 25 years old.
* A group of ibis is called a congregation.
* Their nostrils are at the base of their long beak, which allows them to keep breathing while searching for food in the mud.

Northern Ground-hornbill

Bucorvus abyssinicus
(buk-or-vus ab-is-in-e-kus)

Description

Hornbills are known for being large birds, but the ground-hornbill is much larger than the others, reaching around 130 centimetres long and weighing around 4 kilograms, with lanky legs to help them walk long distances. There are two species of ground-hornbills, each just as unusual as the other. Aside from their slightly different names – the southern ground-hornbill and the northern ground-hornbill – there are also some physical features to distinguish between them. The northern ground-hornbill, for example, has blue and red throat colouration and blue patterning around the eye.

Another factor is their large casques (horns), as northern ground-hornbill casques are more curved and feature extra decorations, such as the large tube shaped addition on top.

Conservation Status

LEAST CONCERN

Due to their wide range and large population size, the northern ground-hornbill is not considered to be in danger of becoming extinct. However, they still face threats, such as becoming prey for large mammals, or disease. They are also occasionally hunted for food by humans or killed because they are considered pests or a symbol of bad luck.

Close Relations

They are related to the helmeted hornbill, found on page 65, and have a similar bony casque.

Diet

Unlike helmeted hornbills, ground-hornbills are predominately carnivorous. Their beaks are not evolved to eat fruits or plants and so they eat mainly insects and spiders, though they have also been seen feeding on reptiles like lizards and snakes, and even on small mammals.

Location/Habitat

As their name suggests, these hornbills will spend most of their time on the ground. They prefer to live in dry and rocky environments. At night, they roost in the holes of trees, rocks or stumps. Since they rely on dry areas, they are found across portions of north-central Africa, for example in parts of Kenya, Uganda, Ethiopia and Somalia.

Fun Facts

→ Northern ground-hornbills mate for life (which is known as monogamy) and can be heard singing duets with their partners, a touching display that has inspired songs in local villages.

→ They have been recorded using their bills to wrestle with one another. This is thought to be a way to practise their hunting techniques rather than an act of aggression.

→ In captivity, they have been found to live up to 40 years old.

→ They are also commonly known as the Abyssinian ground-hornbill.

Bucorvus abyssinicus

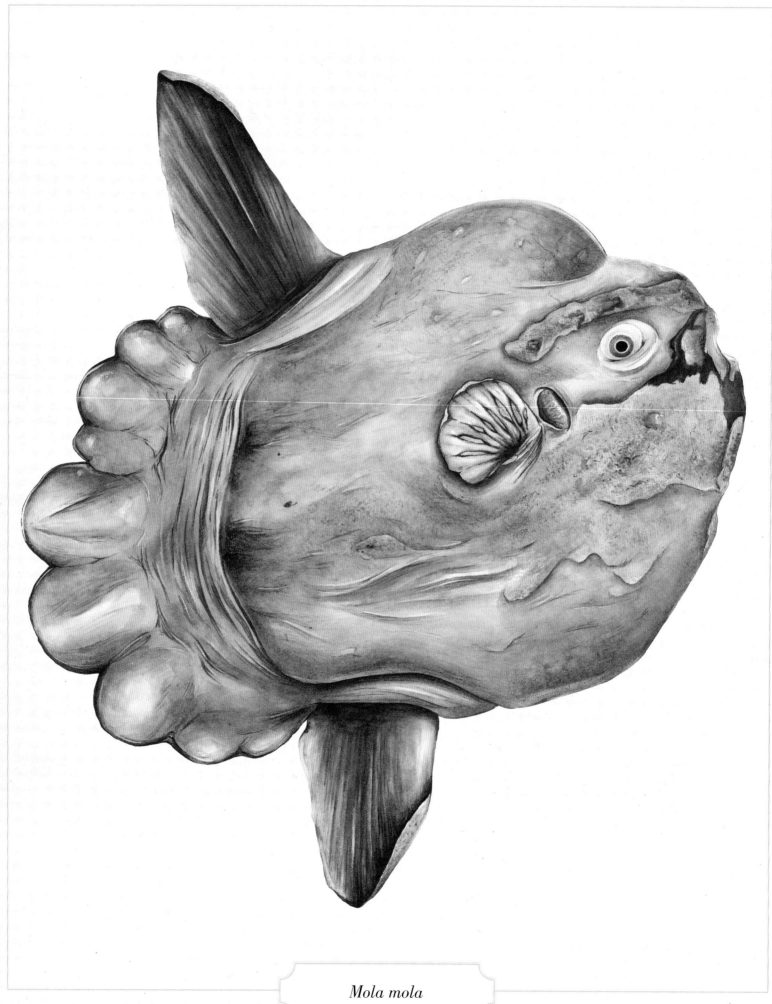

Mola mola

Ocean Sunfish

Mola mola
(mole-a mole-a)

Description

The ocean sunfish is shaped like an enormous pancake. On average, it is 3.5 metres long, 4.2 metres tall and less than 1 metre wide, and weighs around 2.5 tonnes. It does not have a swim bladder like other fish to help control bouyancy but uses a layer of fat instead. This results in the awkward, clumsy fish we know today. The ocean sunfish is the heaviest bony fish in the world.

Conservation Status

VULNERABLE

The ocean sunfish has predators, such as orcas, sea lions and great white sharks.

Humans are the biggest contributor to the sunfish's declining population. Many sunfish are killed by eating plastic, being struck by boats or caught in fishing nets. In one year, it was estimated that 340,000 sunfish were caught, either by accident while attempting to catch other ocean dwellers or on purpose for human consumption.

Close Relations

This enormous fish is closely related to the tiny pufferfish, *Tetraodontidae*.

Diet

Ocean sunfish are omnivorous and eat mostly plankton and jellyfish, and on occasion other fish and crustaceans. Their diet is made up of small animals because their mouths are tiny compared to their large body and they cannot fully close them.

Location/Habitat

Ocean sunfish are found in places as varied as the waters off the central coast of New South Wales in Australia, all the way to the Mediterranean Sea. They spend most of their lives at great depths but sometimes swim to the surface to regulate their body temperature or to use other fish and birds to help rid them of parasites.

Fun Facts

→ They can live for up to 10 years.

→ Their nickname is the 'swimming head'.

→ The scientific name, *Mola mola*, is derived from the Latin translation of 'millstone', which is a grey circular disc used to grind grains and wheat.

→ Their highest-recorded speed is only 3 kilometres per hour.

Proboscis Monkey

Nasalis larvatus

(nay-sa-lis lar-vart-us)

Description

Scientists are unsure about the purpose of the proboscis monkey's long nose. It is thought there is a direct correlation between the size of a male's nose and his attractiveness to females. It is also believed males use their nose to make loud noises which call in potential females, while also warning other males to stay away.

The males weigh around 20 kilograms and can grow to 80 centimetres. The females are smaller, weighing about 10 kilograms and growing to 60 centimetres tall. The females also have a much more petite snout.

Conservation Status

ENDANGERED

Unfortunately, the number of these strange monkeys left in the wild has declined by more than 50% in the last 40 years. Palm oil is the leading cause of this decrease in numbers. Over 7 million hectares of their habitat has been cleared for palm plantations.

Diet

A favourite food of these monkeys is the *Sonneratia caseolaris*, otherwise known as the crabapple mangrove. Proboscis monkeys eat the leaves and also the sour, star-shaped fruit. They also feed on seeds, roots, shoots and, on occasion, insects.

Location/Habitat

Native to Indonesia, Brunei and Malaysia, these mammals live in groups of around 20, with one male and many females. They are arboreal, which means they spend most of their days and nights high in the trees of forests, swamps and mangroves, only coming down to cross the rivers or feed on fallen food.

Fun Facts

→ Proboscis monkeys are very good swimmers, using their webbed hands and feet to assist them when travelling from mangrove to mangrove.

→ The collective noun for a group of proboscis monkeys is a harem.

→ They are a very calm species, rarely fighting each other for dominance.

→ You can help save the proboscis monkey from extinction by monitoring your consumption of palm oil through food, cosmetics and petrol, and by raising awareness about the impact of deforestation.

Nasalis larvatus

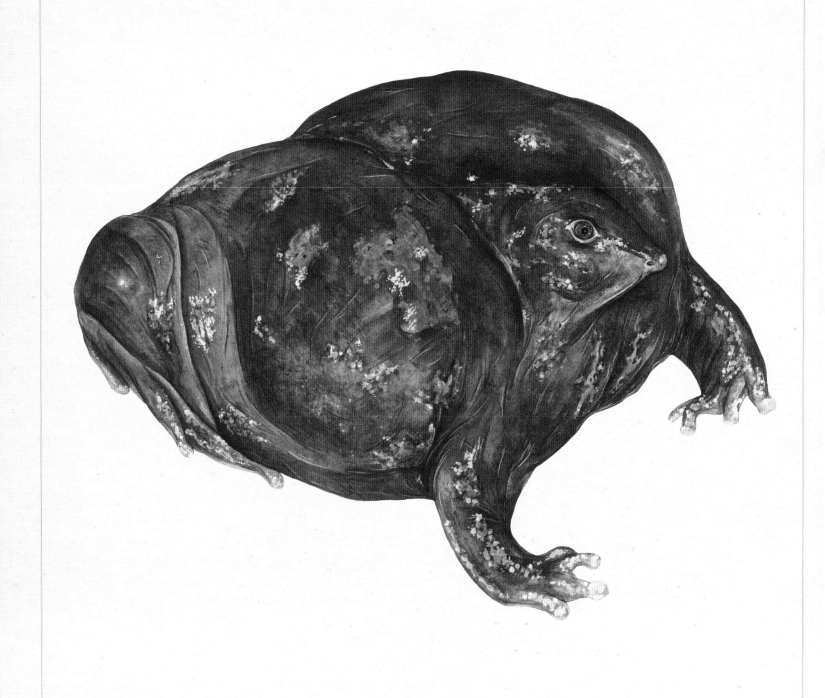

Nasikabatrachus sahyadrensis

Purple Pig-nosed Frog

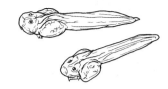

Nasikabatrachus sahyadrensis

(nay-sik-a-bat-rak-us sah-hya-dren-sis)

Description

Purple pig-nosed frogs are only 6–9 centimetres long and 165 grams, with strangely disproportionate bodies and comical expressions. They have small heads and long, hard noses which are perfect for digging through the earth, and their short limbs, which feature a hard knob on the back feet, are ideal for pushing dirt aside. Their mouths are formed so that the lower jaw is flexible and flap-like, allowing their tongue to poke through when feeding.

Conservation Status

ENDANGERED

This bizarre species of frog is extremely rare – only 135 of them have been found in the wild, and only three of these were female! In fact, this species of burrowing frog was not formally recognised by scientists until 2003, despite being known and named by local people. One reason for this is because they are burrowing frogs, rarely seen on land. This also makes it difficult to know the extent of their range and population size and to understand threats to their survival. However, it is thought their biggest threat is deforestation. Ninety per cent of their forest home has been logged – mostly to make way for farm crops like ginger, coffee and cardamom.

Diet

As these frogs spend most of their time underneath the soil, they have adapted some specific traits to assist them with feeding in this environment. A great example of this is their sensitive nose and mouth which are ideal for feeding on small invertebrates and termites. Their tongues are also specially adapted to stick to and suck up these termites, making them very quick eaters.

Location/Habitat

The purple pig-nosed frog can be found in the Western Ghats region of India, in the damp, loose soil of forests and other areas dense with plant life. They spend most of their lives underground as deep as 1 metre. If you are lucky enough to visit during monsoon season, you can spot them in pond-like environments where they spend a few weeks of the year breeding.

Fun Facts

→ Unlike many other frog species, the females are much larger than the males. This is an unusual form of sexual dimorphism.

→ Researchers monitored a frog closely for five months and found it did not emerge from the burrow once in that time!

→ While in its tadpole state, the pig-nosed frog will sometimes crawl out of the water to feed at night, even though it doesn't have any limbs. They get around by using their strong abdominal muscles to assist them in moving from one tiny pocket of water to another.

Red-lipped Batfish

Ogcocephalus darwini

(og-ko-sef-a-lus dar-win-e)

Description

This unique species of batfish is most known for their vibrant red lips, which look like they're covered in freshly applied lipstick. It is not entirely known why they have evolved this feature, but it is thought it might be to attract females during mating season, or to help recognise other batfish.

The red-lipped batfish's elongated snout is thought to be an adaptation to protect the illicium, which is a lure under the nose that wiggles about like a small fish and releases chemicals to draw in nearby prey.

These batfish grow to around 25 centimetres long.

Conservation Status

LEAST CONCERN

Due to the batfish's deep-sea habitat, it is not impacted by environmental changes in the same way as many other oceanic species. Deep-sea trawlers may occasionally drag up these fish or destroy their homes on the seabed, but since they mostly live within the Galápagos Islands Marine Protected Area, their population numbers are stable.

Close Relations

This species is from the same class as the deep-sea anglerfish on page 66. Like anglerfish, they have a fleshy growth called an illicium near their mouth which acts as a lure for prey.

Diet

Their lure assists them in eating large amounts of small fish and invertebrates like crabs, molluscs and shrimp.

Location/Habitat

Found predominantly in the Galápagos Islands, there have also been several accounts of red-lipped batfish appearing in the oceans near Ecuador and Peru. They like to dwell on sandy floors between 3–76 metres below sea level but have been recorded at depths of 120 metres deep.

Fun Facts

→ Instead of swimming to get around, they use their leg-shaped fins to walk across the seabed. They are actually terrible swimmers.

→ Their name is derived from their flat, spread-out body, which is similar to that of a bat.

→ When they become fully grown, their back fin becomes a pointy spike to lure in more prey.

→ They are thought to live to 12 years old.

→ Their scientific name, *darwini*, is in honour of the naturalist Charles Darwin, who developed his theory of evolution after studying animals on the Galápagos Islands.

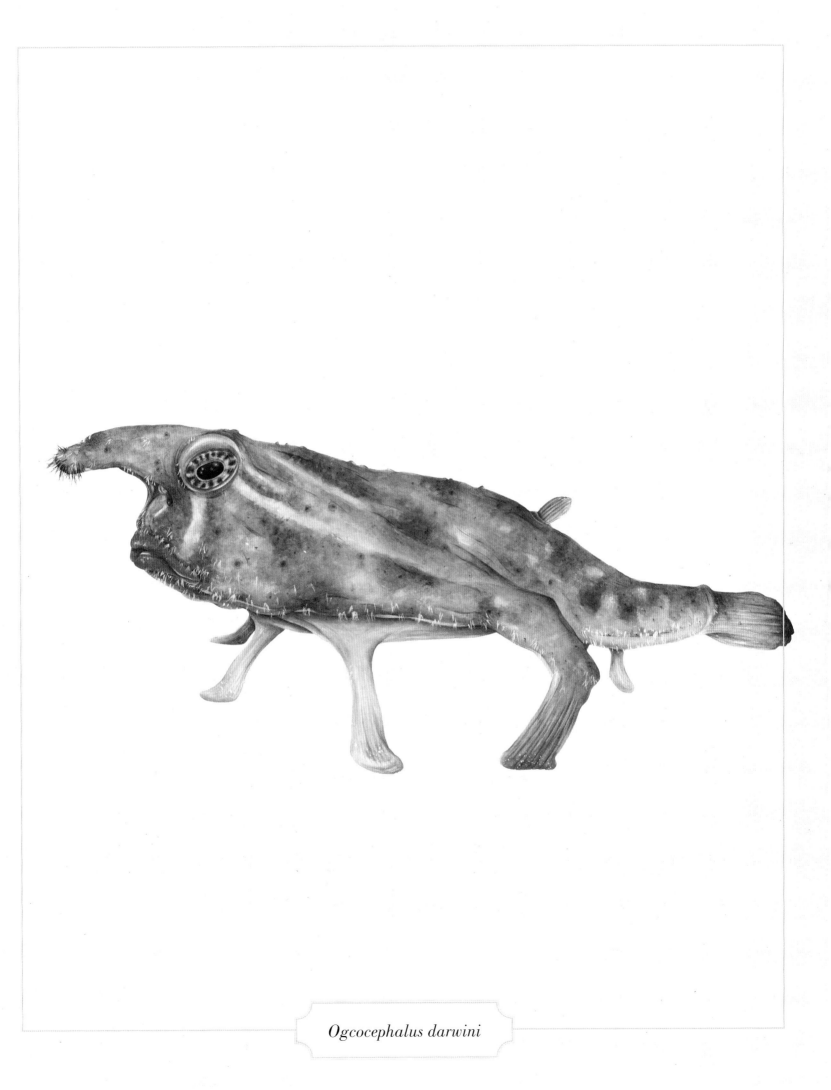

Ogcocephalus darwini

Dactyloscopus foraminosus

Reticulate Stargazer

Dactyloscopus foraminosus
(dak-til-o-sco-pus for-ami-no-sus)

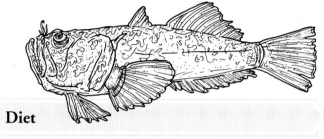

Description

The reticulate stargazer has adapted its form after many years to aid with its survival. This flattened, zombie-faced, speckled fish has eyes on the top of its head and can lay covered on the marine floor and watch its surroundings.

Reaching a maximum of 8 centimetres long, their spotted surface helps them blend in with their surroundings, and their large side-fins are great for digging up the sand around them to cover them in seconds.

Conservation Status

LEAST CONCERN

Reticulate stargazers face very little danger during their lives, as they spend most of their time beneath seabed floors, hidden from any potential threats.

Some fishermen consider the fish to be a luxury, but most keep their distance because the fish has a tendency to sting and electrocute when threatened.

Diet

This unusual fish has evolved some very interesting features to help it hunt and feed on crabs, small fish and squid. It attracts prey with its worm-like lure above its mouth, dangling it around and then lurching forwards to swallow its victims. It uses its zipper-like appendages on the outside of its mouth to stop any unwanted sand and other debris from getting inside.

Location/Habitat

The stargazer species is difficult to come across because of its ability to hide in the sand and gravel of marine waters. If you would like to try your luck finding the reticulate stargazer, it can be found in areas of the Western Atlantic waters, such as the Brazilian coasts, at depths of around 11 metres to 80 metres.

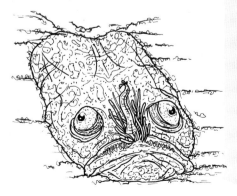

Fun Facts

→ Stargazers have two venomous spines which are used to ward off threats rather than to help it catch prey.

→ They are called stargazers because their eyes face straight upwards and out towards the sky.

→ They will often burp out the scales of fish that they eat.

→ There are nearly 50 different species of stargazers.

→ They feature an organ behind their eyes which can implement an electrical shock of up to 50 volts.

Saiga Antelope

Saiga tatarica

(sigh-ga tat-arik-a)

Description

This unusual creature is one of the most mythical-looking species out there, and at first glance it is hard to believe it is real – it looks like a mix of a deer and an elephant.

The purpose of the saiga antelopes' long snouts is to help them breathe easier and to regulate their body temperature in their very hot and dusty habitat. The larger the nose is, the more efficiently it can cool the body.

Standing at around 70 centimetres tall at shoulder height and weighing approximately 40 kilograms for males and 30 kilograms for females, saiga antelope are timid animals who like to live in small herds when not migrating.

Conservation Status

CRITICALLY ENDANGERED

In the last 40 years, it is thought the population of this unique creature has dropped by over 1,200,000 individuals, leaving only around 50,000 left in the wild – a catastrophic loss. They are now completely extinct in China and Ukraine. Hunters kill male saiga antelope in order to obtain their highly prized meat and horns. This skews the male to female ratio, and affects their breeding habits and population size.

The World Wildlife Fund has listed these critically endangered animals as a priority species in order to try and prevent them becoming entirely extinct.

Diet

Saiga antelope usually eat grass, shrubs, lichen and herbs. Uniquely, they can also eat plants that are deadly to other animals without getting sick.

Location/Habitat

To find these extremely rare mammals, you must travel to Mongolia, Russia or Kazakhstan. Populations are dropping fast and in some places they have not been seen in 40 years. One of the most impressive things about this species of antelope is the enormous and very tiring migration journey they take in November each year. Saiga antelope will travel in numbers of over 10,000 in search of fresh semi-arid deserts with enough low-lying trees and plants. They do not like areas that are too dense as it is more difficult to escape if feeling threatened in such areas.

Fun Facts

→ The heated fights the saiga antelope have during mating seasons can be deadly. The antelopes can cause one another a lot of pain and injury with their horns.

→ They have been recorded to live up to 10 years.

→ These speedy animals are extremely fearful and can run up to 80 kilometres per hour to escape predators.

→ Saiga antelope rely on their keen eyesight to look out for danger. Many other antelope species rely on their hearing.

Saiga tatarica

Chelonoidis darwini

Santiago Giant Tortoise

Chelonoidis darwini

(kel-o-noy-dis dar-win-e)

Description

Giant tortoises are sometimes compared to the small, cute turtles that are seen more commonly, so it is no wonder they are thought to be ugly in comparison.

Their enormous size, dull grey colouring and deep wrinkles covering their neck, head and feet all add up to qualify them for the ugly list.

These tortoises have very long necks, which allow them to reach tall plants and foods, and which are also useful during confrontations with other tortoises. In these clashes, the tortoises face one another with their necks fully extended and their mouths open wide.

Because of the hot temperatures they live in and their minimal food needs, Santiago giant tortoises spend the majority of their time sleeping and resting, sometimes for weeks at a time.

Conservation Status

CRITICALLY ENDANGERED

The Santiago giant tortoise, which once populated the Galápagos Islands well into the nineteenth century, is now on the brink of extinction. When non-native animals like goats, pigs and donkeys were introduced to the Galápagos, they quickly began to destroy the landscape and eat the eggs laid by the tortoises. Eventually, the goats were removed, but this created additional problems because invasive vegetation species, like blackberry bushes, grew out of control and further impacted the tortoises' habitat.

Diet

These incredible animals can last a whole year without food and water. One adaptation that enables them to do this is that they can store water in their bladders. When they do feed, it is usually on grass, fruits and sometimes cactus pads.

Location/Habitat

Native to Ecuador, they can be found on the Galápagos island of Santiago, which was previously known as James Island.

Fun Facts

→ The Santiago giant tortoise can potentially live to over 150 years old!

→ It is suspected that around 2–3 million years ago, the first tortoises arrived on the Galápagos via rafts made from vegetation. Young tortoises would take refuge on these vessels and float away accidentally.

→ The temperature of the sand or soil that eggs have been laid in determines whether the baby tortoises will be female or male.

→ Around 165 years ago, Charles Darwin brought a young Santiago giant tortoise named Harriet from the Galápagos to Australia. Harriet spent part of her life at Australia Zoo. It is thought she was 175 years old when she died there in 2006.

Neoclinus blanchardi

Sarcastic Fringehead

Neoclinus blanchardi
(ne-o-kline-us blan-char-dee)

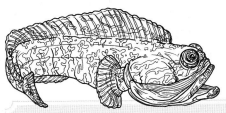

Description

Sarcastic fringeheads aren't creatures you would want to come across while taking a swim. Not only do they have terrifyingly wide mouths filled with needle-sharp teeth, but their personalities are just as frightening as their appearance.

After giving a few warning signs by flashing their large mouth and teeth, sarcastic fringeheads will attack if they think there's still a threat. They'll even attack humans! Because of this fierce behaviour, they have very few predators, despite being relatively small – only around 25 centimetres long.

They use the same technique when competing with other males for a mate and will open their mouth wide to try and dominate by size and show. Sometimes they will lunge at each other, bumping faces to intimidate one another, with the loser retreating.

Conservation Status

LEAST CONCERN

Similar to the red-lipped batfish on page 98, this underwater species spends its days far down in the ocean where it is very rarely caught by fishermen or trawlers and water pollutants have less impact. Since the fringehead also happens to live in protected areas, its population is not considered to be at risk.

Diet

This omnivorous fish's diet is not well documented due to its deep-sea nature, but it is thought that they feed on small plankton, fish, crustaceans, squid and their eggs.

Location/Habitat

Sarcastic fringeheads enjoy the subtropical climates of the eastern Pacific Ocean and live off the coast of California and Mexico. They spend their time on sandy or muddy sea floors, at depths as low as 60 metres, and like to rest in burrows or large shells made from other animals.

Fun Facts

➢ Sarcastic fringeheads have been seen to reside in plastic bottles or other rubbish that has made its way into the ocean.

➢ Their unusual name comes from the original Greek meaning of 'sarcastic', which is 'to tear flesh'.

➢ Fishermen are not likely to fish for these fringeheads because of their aggressive nature.

➢ They consume 13.6 times their body weight in food per year.

➢ Females lay their eggs in burrows dug out by other animals and which have since been abandoned, and the males stand guard to protect the eggs from any hungry visitors.

Sea Lamprey

Petromyzon marinus

(petro-my-zon ma-reen-us)

Description

These 1-metre-long, 2.5-kilogram snake-like creatures are often mistaken for eels when swimming through the water. The major difference between the two is that lampreys have circular mouths filled with rows of large teeth. This formation helps them feed in their unusual manner – sea lampreys will attach themselves to other fish and suck up their host's blood and nutrients. This is known as being parasitic.

Conservation Status

LEAST CONCERN

Conservation status is an interesting matter in the case of the sea lamprey. They are seen as a pest by many because of their negative impact on other fish, particularly those that are traded across the globe.

This is the only 'ugly' animal in this book that has an official program in place to decrease their numbers, with traps set up in the Great Lakes region of North America to prevent any further damage to other fish numbers.

Diet

Some of the sea lamprey's favourite prey are catfish, salmon and rainbow trout, and a single lamprey will kill around 18.2 kilograms of these fish per year. They spend most of their days in groups attaching to different hosts,

but once they reach sexual maturity, they stop feeding altogether.

Location/Habitat

The sea lamprey is a migrating species and has been recorded to travel from salt oceans to freshwater lakes and streams. In adulthood, they travel to spawning streams in order to reproduce. This is an unusual ability and very few species can survive through such different salinity levels.

Sea lampreys can be found throughout the Atlantic Ocean, in areas surrounding Iceland and in the western Mediterranean Sea. They have also been introduced to many other regions, causing destruction as they pass through.

Fun Facts

> Their other common names are spotted lamprey and green lamprey.

> Sea lampreys can reach five years of age.

> They have a cartilaginous skeleton, meaning they are made entirely of cartilage rather than bone.

> A female lamprey can lay between 30,000 to 100,000 eggs when spawning.

> Young lampreys are blind and do not have teeth.

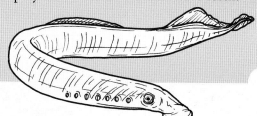

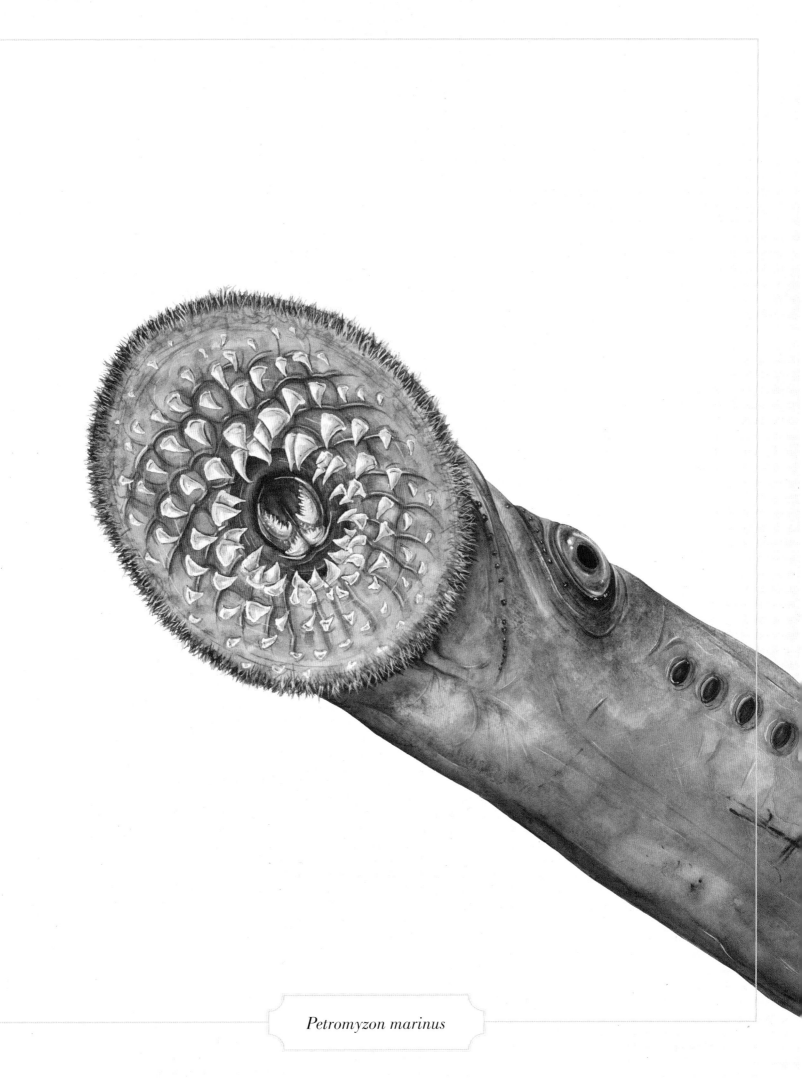

Petromyzon marinus

Casuarius casuarius

Southern Cassowary

Casuarius casuarius

(cas-oo-ary-us cas-oo-ary-us)

Description

The southern cassowary has a large, horn-like helmet, otherwise known as a casque, which is surprisingly soft inside. This adaptation evolved to assist them when pushing through the dense rainforest foliage and begins to grow at one or two years of age.

The purpose of the two dangling red wattles on their necks is unclear. It is believed they can intensify in colour when the bird is enraged or disturbed, which is a useful warning sign for other cassowaries or people. Weighing in at 76 kilograms, the females are heavier than the males, and can grow to 2 metres tall. The males only get to around 55 kilograms.

Conservation Status

LEAST CONCERN

The southern cassowary doesn't have many predators, except for dogs and feral pigs. Their dropping numbers are largely due to car collisions, being hunted for meat and their habitat being cleared for logging and palm oil plantations.

Diet

These large birds feed predominately on fallen fruit and fungi, and it is because of this that they are known as the best seed distributors of the rainforest. They poo out the seeds from the fruits they eat, helping plant new trees and bushes. They also occasionally feed on small animals like snails and fish.

Location/Habitat

The southern cassowary is native to Australia, eastern Indonesia and Papua New Guinea, but you have the best chance of seeing it in the wild around rainforest climates in northern Queensland, Australia. They can occasionally be found on beaches, and in mangroves, woodlands and swamps.

Fun Facts

→ The southern cassowary is the heaviest non-flying bird in Australia.

→ Because of their powerful legs, they can run at speeds of 50 kilometres per hour and jump 1.5 metres high.

→ The males sit on the eggs to warm and protect them.

→ One of the easiest ways to determine whether a bird is male or female is to measure the size of its feet. A female's feet are over 21 centimetres long and a male's are shorter.

→ The cassowary plum, *Cerbera floribunda*, is named after the bird for two reasons: it is one of its favourite foods and it features the same vibrant blue colour that makes the southern cassowary iconic.

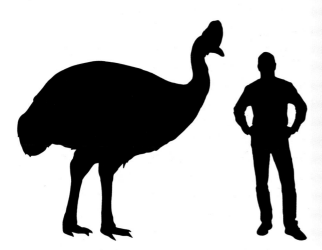

Southern Elephant Seal

Mirounga leonina
(mi-rung-ga leo-ni-na)

Description

One of the most incredible things about southern elephant seals is the enormous sizes they can reach. Females can grow to 800 kilograms and 4 metres long while males can reach a massive 4,000 kilograms and 6 metres long! This makes them the largest carnivore living today.

Another amazing physical feature is their funny, trunk-like nose, which overhangs their face by about 10 centimetres. This trunk doubles as an amplifier when it is inflated, allowing their calls to be heard far and wide. Males will also make bellowing sounds during fights and dominance displays, to help prove which male is boss.

In order to defend their harems, the males will stay on their territory without leaving. This can last for months on end, and because they are not able to leave and find food, their energy and condition suffer greatly. This ensures that only the strongest males are able to breed and pass on their genes.

Conservation Status

LEAST CONCERN

Around 30 years ago, the population of the southern elephant seal was around 650,000 individuals across the globe. It is thought this number dropped due to the effects of climate change and overfishing. Other, more natural, threats are few and far between due to the enormous size of these seals. They are sometimes hunted by killer whales, great white sharks and leopard seals, who mainly prey on the smaller pups. Other elephant seals also pose a risk as they can injure one another in fights.

Diet

Because of their build, southern elephant seals can hunt and eat large animals. However, it is difficult to know the full extent of their diet because they feed while out at sea. It is thought they eat animals like sharks, large fish, squid and even mysterious and rarely seen deep-sea creatures.

Location/Habitat

These mammals are native to the coasts of Antarctica and subantarctic islands, but they have also been recorded a handful of times in Australia, New Zealand and South Africa. This range is only an estimate because it is extremely difficult to know where females, who spend most of their time at sea, go outside of the mating season.

Fun Facts

- Southern elephant seals are expected to live up to 23 years.
- They have been recorded holding their breath for up to two hours!
- It is thought this species of seal has existed for one million years.
- Even though they can travel up to 5,000 kilometres away to find good feeding waters, elephant seals will return to the place they were born in order to breed.
- Prior to 1964, elephant seals were hunted for their blubber, which was used for oil.

Mirounga leonina

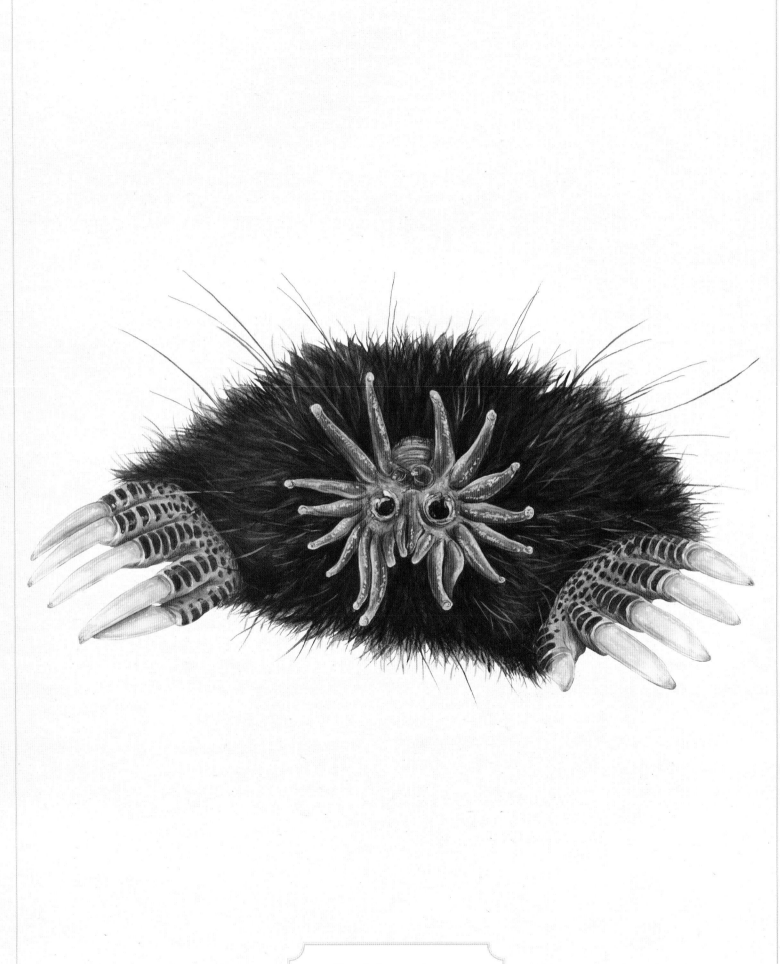

Condylura cristata

Star-nosed Mole

Condylura cristata
(con-de-lure-a cris-ta-ta)

Description

The star-nosed mole, like its name suggests, has a star-shaped nose which features 22 points. The purpose of this ugly nose is to assist them in searching for prey and in knowing where to dig their tunnels. Their noses are packed with over 25,000 sensory elements known as 'Eimer's organs'. Because the moles have such terrible eyesight, these tiny features on the skin of their nose are incredibly useful in helping them feel around different objects. The moles can sense the microscopic texture of everything they touch to determine exactly what the object is. In doing this, the nose moves around so quickly that it touches up to 12 objects per second.

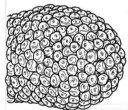

The star-nosed mole grows to between 17.5 and 20 centimetres long, with a 7-millimetre-long tail, covered in scales and course hair.

Conservation Status

LEAST CONCERN

Star-nosed moles have a few natural predators such as fish, bullfrogs and large birds, like owls. They are also under threat from more invasive species like domesticated cats and dogs, and suffer from the effects of human expansion into their environment. However, these hazards do not impact their population size enough to put them at risk of extinction.

Close Relations

This species is related to the naked mole rat, featured on page 85, and also lives in long, sophisticated tunnel networks.

Diet

You would probably expect the star-nosed mole's nose to have some use when feeding, but it is only helpful in finding prey and serves no purpose at all when the mole is eating. Fortunately, it doesn't get in the way either. In fact, these moles are the world's fastest eaters. They can demolish foods like worms, insects, fish and crustaceans in just a quarter of a second!

Location/Habitat

These creepy critters are native to the north-eastern states of the US but can also be found in parts of Canada, ranging further north than any other species of mole. They like to inhabit wetter areas, such as the clearings and meadows surrounding riverbanks, lakes and ponds.

To find them, you will need to look for a mole hill, which is a mound of dirt created outside their tunnels and made from all the dirt they have dug out. Their intricate network of tunnels can reach 270 metres long.

Fun Facts

- While star-nosed moles wade through and swim underwater, they are able to blow out air bubbles from their nose and re-inhale them. This incredible ability lets them take in the surrounding smells and helps them locate their prey.
- The collective noun for a group of moles is a 'labour'.
- Their Eimer's organs are filled with so many sensory nerves that their nose is five times more sensitive than the human hand.

Surinam Toad

Pipa pipa
(pip-a pip-a)

Description

If you have trypophobia – a fear of small, tightly packed holes (like in a lotus head or seeds on the outside of a strawberry) – then look away from the Surinam toad now. They're covered in them! These bizarre toads looks like they have been stepped on and flattened. Males average around 10–15 centimetres long and females are about 10–17 centimetres. They have developed a peculiar yet incredible trait: the ability to grow and hatch babies on their backs. This adaptation means that they can protect their eggs from predators, which they could not do so well if they laid the eggs on a rock or in the water.

During mating, eggs are implanted in the female's back and afterwards, she grows a layer of skin over them. Tiny toads emerge from her back after 12–20 weeks.

Conservation Status

LEAST CONCERN

Surinam toads are occasionally taken from their habitats and used in the pet trade, but the main threat to their numbers is habitat loss and destruction.

Although they live in many protected areas, they still fall victim to logging, plantations and an intruding human population. Fortunately, they still have large numbers and are not at risk of becoming extinct in the near future.

Diet

Unlike most frogs and toads, the Surinam toad does not have a tongue. When feeding, it relies on its stretched-out, star-like fingers to sense food on the riverbed, grab it and pile it into its mouth.

Surinam toads usually find worms, small fish, invertebrates and crustaceans through this clever technique, but they are not fussy eaters and will gobble almost anything they come across. Even other Surinam toads!

Location/Habitat

This toad gets its name from one of its native locations, Suriname. They are also spotted in places like Bolivia, Ecuador, Colombia, Brazil, and Trinidad and Tobago, as well as some other places in the Amazon basin of South America. They can be difficult to spot as they are extremely flat and camouflage well into their environment, tucked under leaves or dirt in the ponds, rivers and pools of water in rainforests.

Fun Facts

- They have small, fleshy flaps in the corners of their mouths which act like a lure for prey, similar to the anglerfish on page 66.
- Babies that emerge from a female's back are not tadpoles. They are mini-adults and are fully independent.
- Although toads in captivity sometimes eat one another and need to be separated, they do not eat their own babies.
- Surinam toads have developed eyes which allow them to look in every direction and stay alert to their surroundings.

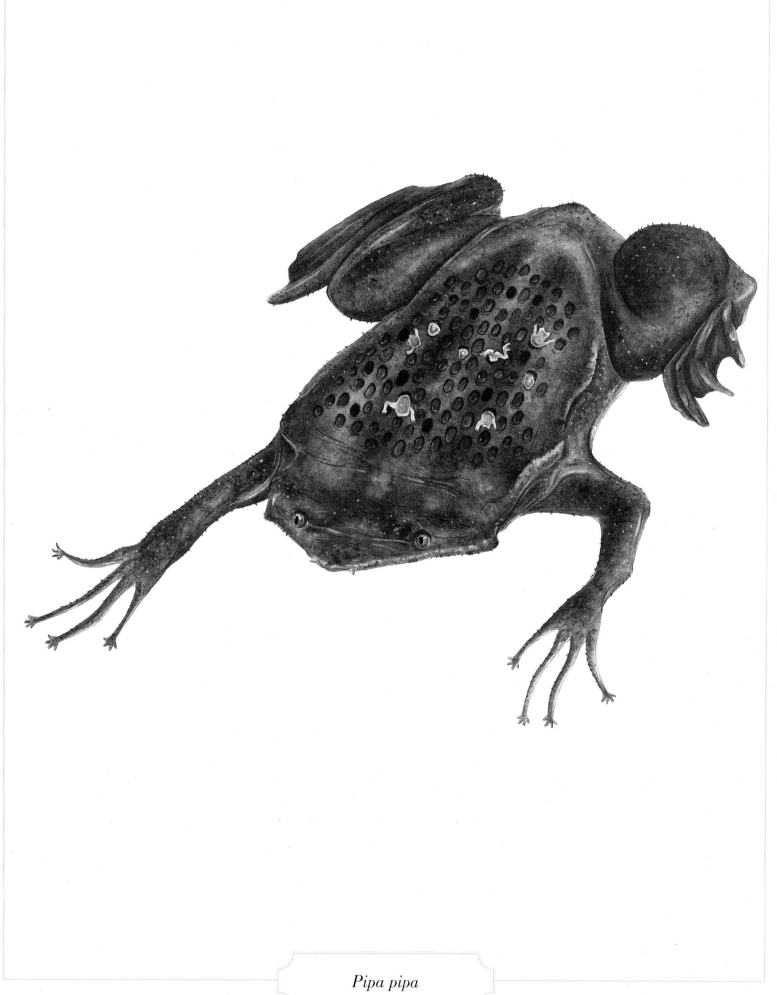

Pipa pipa

Tardigrada

Tardigrade

Tardigrada

(tar-di-grad-a)

Description

All 1,000 known species of these weird-looking invertebrates are so small – measuring only 0.05–1.2 millimetres – that you cannot see them with the naked eye. They have a barrel-shaped body and four pairs of stubby legs.

They are able to self-fertilise, otherwise known as hermaphroditism, which comes in useful if they are unable to find a mate.

Conservation Status

NOT EVALUATED

Since this creature is so minuscule, it is nearly impossible to find out its range and population, so it has not been evaluated for conservation purposes. Its size also means that it has very few threats, with its only suspected predators being slightly larger creatures like spiders, crustaceans, mites, snails and other tardigrades.

Other threats include the changes to their habitats caused by climate change.

Diet

Their tube-like mouth is filled with sharp teeth that are used to suck the juices from the cells of moss, algae and bacteria. They are even known to feast on fellow tardigrades.

0.05-1.2 millimetres

Location/Habitat

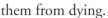

These astonishing creatures have adapted to survive in conditions that many of us could never dream of. For example, they can survive in extreme temperatures from a freezing -272 degrees up to the scorching heat of 149 degrees Celsius. Believe it or not, they can even survive in space by placing their bodies in a state of inactivity known as cryptobiosis, which prevent them from dying.

Distributed across the world, tardigrade can be found in all sorts of semi-aquatic and aquatic environments from the Arctic to the Antarctic.

Fun Facts

- Their colour depends on their diet.
- They are also known as moss piglets and water bears.
- A specimen was discovered to have survived over 30 years in its dormant state.
- It is thought that a tardigrade can usually live between 3 months and 2.5 years.
- These animals are so resilient, they have survived five mass extinctions over the last 5 hundred million years.

Turkey Vulture

Cathartes aura

(kath-art or-a)

Description

This enormous bald bird has a massive wingspan of nearly 2 metres, yet only weighs 1.5–2 kilograms. While it may look strange, with its dense feathers covering its whole body except for its head, there is a very good reason for its baldness.

When feeding on carrion, turkey vultures can often get quite messy, but it would be a waste of time and effort to clean feathers on their heads because they would only get dirty again at their next mealtime. It's a good thing these birds evolved bare heads!

Conservation Status

LEAST CONCERN

The turkey vulture has a very unusual way of deterring predators. If threatened, they will throw up their last meal (which is almost always old, rotting meat). This gives off such a strong odour that other animals are completely deterred. Because of this, they face few natural predators. Humans are the leading cause of death in this species, through trapping, shooting or car accidents.

Diet

What might taste revolting to humans is what appeals most to turkey vultures who, like marabou storks (on page 78), eat mostly carrion. This means they feed on animals that are already dead and have often started to decay. This can include roadkill, cattle and smaller birds. Sometimes they will eat insects and fruits.

It might sound gross, but scavenger birds are extremely important to our ecosystem because they clean up decaying and germ-ridden animal bodies that would otherwise contaminate the area.

Location/Habitat

Turkey vultures travel long distances to find food so it's hard to know exactly where they live. It is thought that they mainly inhabit parts of Canada, Chile and areas in the United States like Texas and Minnesota. Where they roost depends on where they are feeding at the time, and it can vary from forests to flat environments, in trees, cliffs or even man-made structures.

Fun Facts

- As well as throwing up to frighten away potential threats, turkey vultures will also play dead – though this only works if the other animal isn't a scavenger!
- If you want to avoid being thrown up on, you can tell a turkey vulture is threatened because it will make a hissing sound.
- They have a keen sense of smell and use it to locate dead animals rather than relying purely on sight.
- Turkey vultures form strong bonds with their mates and two birds will remain together for life.
- They have been seen to sleep in flocks as large as a few hundred birds, probably for the safety in numbers.

Cathartes aura

Acryllium vulturinum

Vulturine Guineafowl

Acryllium vulturinum
(a-krill-e-um vul-chur-e-num)

Description

These birds have what appears at first sight to be a receding, spiky hairstyle, but is actually thought to be an adaptation useful in helping the birds choose a mate.

They get their name from their featherless head which makes them look a lot like bald-headed vultures, who are bald so that they can feed on carcases without their head feathers becoming filthy. However, vulturine guineafowls eat a predominately plant-based diet, so they have no reason to shield their head from blood or mess.

Both sexes are between 60 and 72 centimetres tall and weigh between 10 and 16 kilograms, so it can be difficult to tell them apart. One way to tell is that males can be seen fighting one another over food, mates and territory. They also carry themselves differently, trying to look as large and intimidating as possible to frighten off the competition.

Conservation Status

LEAST CONCERN

There are few threats to this species of guineafowl, and so they are relatively plentiful.

They do, however, have a small number of predators, for example other, larger, birds, as well as monkeys and pigs, which feed on their eggs. Humans also like to hunt vulturine guineafowl for their

vibrant blue feathers, which are sought after for decorative purposes.

Diet

The shape of their beaks means they are best suited to feeding on vegetation like grass, leaves, roots, fruits and seeds. Sometimes they eat insects, small reptiles and scorpions, which they dig up from the ground with their sharp claws.

Location/Habitat

To see this bird in its natural habitat, you must go to eastern Africa, where they can be found in the tropical areas of Kenya, Ethiopia, Somalia, Uganda and Tanzania.

They enjoy humid lowland forests and dry grasslands and live in large groups of around 25 individuals for safety in numbers.

Fun Facts

- Although they have wings, vulturine guineafowls prefer to walk or run across the ground, even if they are bothered or scared.
- They live to around 15 years of age.
- Usually females will share nests, lay their eggs together and help each other with their duties.
- They are the tallest of all guineafowl species.
- Because of their high plant intake, they usually don't need to drink water – they can get all the liquid they need from the plants.

Whitemargin Unicornfish

Naso annulatus

(nay-so an-you-la-tus)

Description

As you may have guessed, the unicornfish gets its name from a long proboscis on its head. The exact purpose of this feature is unknown, but it will begin to grow once the fish has reached approximately 20 centimetres long. The 'horn' will grow to lengths of 13 centimetres and the fish's body will reach a maximum length of 1 metre.

This species is sexually dimorphic, and the males have much longer features than the females.

Conservation Status

LEAST CONCERN

Whitemargin unicornfish are targeted for their meat in the Philippines and also occasionally taken to be sold in aquariums. As a result, their population and distribution has been adversely affected over the years. However, this impact has been minimal, and they remain of least concern in terms of conservation.

Close Relations

They are part of the surgeonfish family and so are related to Dory from *Finding Nemo*.

Diet

These herbivorous fish will use their small, sharp teeth to gnaw off the algae that quickly cover coral and rocks in the ocean, which is incredibly useful because this algae can overgrow and kill the coral it grows on.

They also eat tiny plankton littered throughout the ocean.

Location/Habitat

Found at depths of 20–60 metres, the whitemargin unicornfish inhabits tropical waters throughout the Indo-Pacific region and is often found in schools feeding on coral and reefs of the warmer waters. They can also be found all along the Great Barrier Reef, Lord Howe Island and other areas off the coast of Australia.

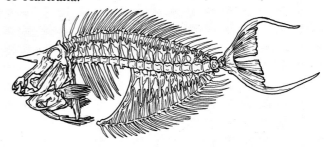

Fun Facts

> Whitemargin unicornfish have been recorded to reach the ripe old age of 23!

> Although they are known as whitemargin unicornfish, they can actually change their colour depending on their mood.

> They also go by the names ringtail unicornfish and short-horned unicornfish.

> At the base of their tails, they have extremely sharp spines which are used in self-defence and in dominance displays between males.

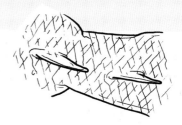

Naso annulatus

Meleagris gallopavo

Wild Turkey

Meleagris gallopavo
(mel-e-a-gris gal-o-parv-o)

Description

Male and female wild turkeys are quite different in appearance, with the males displaying incredible iridescent feathers, wrinkled skin hanging down from their throats, spurs on their legs which they use in combat and a strange projection on their beak and heads (known as a 'wattle', 'snood' or 'caruncle'). This 'ugly' facial feature has a very specific purpose – it inflates and changes colour from red to blue depending on how the bird is feeling – for example, if it is threatened or angry, or if it is looking to mate. Males can reach 6.8–11 kilograms, while female turkeys – which are called hens – usually weigh only 3.6–5.4 kilograms and are brown with a feathered neck.

Only male turkeys gobble. They use the sound to attract females for mating and to ward off any competing males.

Conservation Status

LEAST CONCERN

The wild turkey is the most popular game bird species in the United States and a key element of Thanksgiving dinner. Each year, over 45 million birds are killed in the US alone. There has been a 18,700% increase in the wild turkey population over the last 40 years. They were reintroduced, with significant success, after disappearing in many regions due to excessive hunting. Other than humans, wild turkeys are also threatened by foxes, racoons, snakes and rodents, who will all happily feast on them or their eggs.

Diet

Like other species of turkey, the wild turkey is an omnivore and will use their feet to scratch away at foliage on the ground, searching for insects, nuts, seeds and leaves. Sometimes they will even reach up to short trees and shrubs to peck off buds and fruits.

Location/Habitat

Wild turkeys can be found in forests, woodlands, pastures and fields, where they will spend most of their day grazing before roosting together in trees at night for protection. You can find these turkeys throughout parts of the United States, Canada and Mexico, but they have also been introduced to New Zealand, Australia and Germany.

Fun Facts

➤ Wild turkeys can potentially reach as old as 10 years but due to their popularity as food for humans, most only live for 5–6 months.

➤ Their gobbles can be heard as far as 1.5 kilometres away.

➤ This species has been known to lay their eggs in other birds' nests, a practice known as egg dumping. This frees the adults from having to incubate their eggs themselves.

➤ Chicks are independent 24 hours after they are born. They can walk and even feed themselves!

➤ Wild turkeys are often riddled with disease and parasites, however most are not thought to be transferable to humans or mammals.

About the author

Sami Bayly is a natural history illustrator based in Newcastle, Australia, who loves all things weird and wonderful. She finds the beauty in all animals regardless of their appearance, and hopes to share her appreciation with others.

The Illustrated Encyclopaedia of 'Ugly' Animals is her first book.

To keep up to date you can follow Sami on Instagram
 @samibayly

Teachers' notes and a full list of references can be found at
www.hachette.com.au/sami-bayly/the-illustrated-encyclopaedia-of-ugly-animals